PRAISE FOR
happy herbivore abroad

"In Lindsay Nixon's new cookbook, *Happy Herbivore Abroad*, you'll find delicious, healthful, low-fat recipes from around the world. Travel to France, Mexico, India, Vietnam, Lebanon, and more without leaving your kitchen. If you are looking to transition to a vegan diet or add more creative plant-based foods, this is the cookbook for you."

—Neal Barnard, M.D., president, Physicians Committee for Responsible Medicine

"In *Happy Herbivore Abroad*, Lindsay shows there are truly no limits to plant-based eating. She has collected the most iconic recipes from around the world and made them completely accessible, absolutely delicious, and plant perfect."

—Caldwell B. Esselstyn, Jr., M.D., *New York Times* bestselling author, *Prevent and Reverse Heart Disease*

"The latest in the Happy Herbivore series captures tasty cuisine from around the world and brings it to the table in way that is both healthy and easy-to-prepare."

—Brian Wendel, executive producer, *Forks Over Knives*

"Lindsay has provided easy-to-prepare recipes with readily available ingredients in this worldly view of eating and enjoying a low-fat tasty vegan diet (McDougall-style). We recommend you add the 'abroad' edition to your Happy Herbivore book collection."

—John and Mary McDougall, The McDougall Program

"Lindsay is on a roll! Her third book, *Happy Herbivore Abroad*, is a culinary treasure with stellar recipes from around the world."

—Mark Reinfeld, executive chef, VeganFusion.com; award-winning author, The 30-Minute Vegan series

"Lindsay Nixon is one of the few plant-based chefs who writes cookbooks that meet all of my criteria—her recipes are plant-based, low-fat, easy-to-make, inexpensive, and, very important, delicious! Her latest, *Happy Herbivore Abroad*, features interesting dishes that are different than the standard plant-based fare and can be enjoyed by everyone, including those who have not yet adopted a plant-based diet. The descriptions of her travels added to the book's appeal; I found myself dreaming of enjoying sumptuous meals in faraway places. A must-have for everyone's kitchen!"

—Pamela A. Popper, Ph. D., N.D., executive director, The Wellness Forum

"*Happy Herbivore Abroad* takes the mystery out of international flavors and brings delectable, low-fat, budget-friendly food, with incredibly accessible ingredients from around the world to your kitchen table."

—Alicia C. Simpson, author of *Quick and Easy Vegan Comfort Food*

"This book makes food as thrilling as traveling!"

—Jane Esselstyn, R.N.

"Lindsay's latest cookbook takes you around the world on a culinary plant-strong adventure! It is packed with healthy, nutritious, and most of all delicious recipes that will help you become your healthiest. Your favorite cuisines from around the world just got a new healthy twist! Like Lindsay's first two cookbooks, *Happy Herbivore Abroad* uses everyday ingredients and combines them into making plant-strong masterpieces."

—Rip Esselstyn, *New York Times* bestselling author, *The Engine 2 Diet*

HAPPY HERBIVORE
abroad

A TRAVELOGUE & OVER 135 FAT-FREE & LOW-FAT VEGAN RECIPES FROM AROUND THE WORLD

Lindsay S. Nixon

BenBella Books, Inc.
Dallas, Texas

BenBella Books, Inc.
10300 N. Central Expressway
Suite #400
Dallas, TX 75231
www.benbellabooks.com
Send feedback to feedback@benbellabooks.com

Printed in the United States of America
10 9 8 7 6 5 4 3 2 1

Library of Congress Cataloging-in-Publication Data is available for this title.
978-1-937856-04-5

Copyediting by Nichelle Nicholes
Proofreading by Cape Cod Compositors, Debra Manette, and Kristin Vorce
Indexing by WordCo Indexing Services, Inc.
Cover design, text design, and composition by Amy Sly
Photographs on pages viii, 2, 16, 19, 65, 76, 79, 80, 97, 110, 122, 131, 135, 154, 175, 196, 214, 215, 219, 251, 252, 256, 277, 282, 300, 309, front cover (top right, two top left), back cover (top left, bottom left, second from the top right), and cover spine by Kel Elwood Photography
Photograph on page 85 by Bigstock
All other photographs by Lindsay S. Nixon
Printed by Versa Press, Inc.

Distributed by Perseus Distribution
perseusdistribution.com
To place orders through Perseus Distribution:
Tel: 800-343-4499
Fax: 800-351-5073
E-mail: orderentry@perseusbooks.com

Significant discounts for bulk sales are available. Please contact Glenn Yeffeth at glenn@benbellabooks.com or 214-750-3628.

to scott & courtney

table of contents

introduction

a word from lindsay

In the last 10 years, I have lived in eight states, visited 46 of them, spent a year as an expat on an island in the Caribbean, and traveled to more than 35 places abroad. As you might imagine, I get tripped up anytime someone asks where I am from—what is my hometown? The truth is, the world is my home and I am celebrating my jet-setter lifestyle in this cookbook. Inside, you will find international recipes and stories of my adventures— but no wacky, hard-to-find ingredients or complex cooking methods. Get a world of taste without the fuss!

As with my last two cookbooks, my recipes are still made with wholesome "everyday" ingredients and without added fats like oil. Join me for a healthy culinary journey throughout the world with a few American classics as our last stop. *Bon appétit!*

why eat vegan?

Eating a plant-based, vegan diet is the fastest-growing food trend, and for good reason. The more plant-based meals we eat, the more benefits we will feel and bestow. Whenever someone asks me why I eat this way, I reply, "For my health, the animals, the environment, my pocketbook . . . and for you."

HEALTH Plant-based (vegan) meals contain zero dietary cholesterol, which is great news for your heart. Vegan meals also tend to contain more fiber, are lower in calories, and center around nutritious foods like beans, grains, vegetables, and fruits. Studies have also shown that eating a plant-based diet can prevent and reverse devastating diseases like hypertension, diabetes, and cancer.

WALLET Staples like beans and rice plus seasonal fruits and vegetables are a bargain in comparison to meat and dairy. Moreover, eating healthfully will save you on health-care costs in the long run!

ANIMALS The lives and deaths of farm animals are often horrifyingly brutal, both physically and psychologically. As a consumer picking up the end product, it's easy to be oblivious rather than conscious.

ENVIRONMENT A plant-based diet is the most eco-friendly and sustainable way we can eat.

HUMANITY It has been said that if the world went vegetarian, we would almost immediately end world hunger. One acre of land can produce either 20,000 pounds of potatoes or a measly 165 pounds of meat.

my story I was a vegetarian for most of my childhood out of a love for animals—I was eating a burger one day in the car as we drove past grazing cows and when I put it together, that was that. But I fell into a meat-eating lifestyle in my teens due to peer pressure. A serious health scare in my early twenties brought me back to a vegetarian diet, and I adopted a plant-based diet the following year.

After reading *The China Study*, *Eat to Live*, and *Skinny Bitch*, I knew I could never go back to vegetarianism. I made my vegan regimen permanent, with a new addition: a diet that not only cut out meat, dairy, and eggs, but one that was low-fat and based on whole foods.

why fat-free & low-fat?

Like many others, my husband and I both struggled with our weight and health for years. In 2007, I adopted a low-fat, no-added-fat vegan diet, and Scott joined me shortly thereafter. In the span of a year, we both lost more weight than we previously thought possible and reversed or eliminated all of our medical conditions. We also noticed a surge in our energy levels and went on to complete our first marathon, something that never seemed realistic or possible before.

We all know about the dangers of hydrogenated oils, but other oils, like olive oil, can also be harmful. Most "cooking oils," such as canola oil, have very low burning points. When these oils are heated beyond that boiling point, the nutrients are lost and free radicals are created. Oils are also sneaky calorie bombs, both high in fat and high in calories. One tablespoon of oil has approximately 120 calories and 14g of fat—the same as a candy bar!

To obtain essential fatty acids, I eat unprocessed fats, such as nuts and seeds, sparingly. Also remember that all foods, even greens, naturally contain a little fat, so the body is always getting plenty of fat without adding extra.

The nutritional information for each recipe was computed using caloriecount.com. Each analysis provided is per serving. Unless otherwise noted, optional ingredients are not included. Breads and wraps are also not included, unless specifically noted (see packaging for that information). Sodium content is not included because the value changes significantly between brands and the calculator tools have too much discrepancy with sodium to provide a safe estimate.

getting started

When writing this cookbook, I lived in a Colorado ski town (population: 12,000) and found the majority of these ingredients at our chain supermarket, but a handful of ingredients did require a trip to the health food store. You can also buy many ingredients online, often at lower prices. My favorite websites are bulkfoods.com, vitacost.com, and Amazon.

If any ingredient is unfamiliar to you, look it up in the Glossary of Ingredients (pg. 288).

SHOPPING LIST

Below is my basic shopping list. If you have these ingredients on hand, you can make pretty much any recipe in this cookbook. I also recommend buying organic, no-salt-added, and unsweetened options whenever possible.

pantry

- ☐ agave nectar
- ☐ baking powder
- ☐ baking soda
- ☐ brown rice
- ☐ brown sugar
- ☐ canned beans (assortment)
- ☐ canned green chilis (diced)
- ☐ canned pineapple
- ☐ canned pureed pumpkin
- ☐ canned tomatoes (diced)
- ☐ chickpea flour
- ☐ cornmeal
- ☐ cornstarch
- ☐ instant and rolled oats

- ☐ lentils
- ☐ lite coconut milk
- ☐ quinoa
- ☐ raisins
- ☐ refried beans
- ☐ raw sugar
- ☐ silken tofu (e.g., Mori-Nu)
- ☐ tomato paste
- ☐ tomato sauce
- ☐ unsweetened applesauce
- ☐ unsweetened cocoa
- ☐ vanilla extract
- ☐ vegan chocolate chips
- ☐ vegetable broth
- ☐ vital wheat gluten

□ white whole-wheat flour
□ whole-wheat or gluten-free pasta

condiments

□ balsamic vinegar
□ brown rice vinegar
□ dijon mustard
□ hot sauce
□ ketchup
□ low-sodium soy sauce
□ pure maple syrup

□ red wine vinegar
□ salsa
□ smooth peanut butter
□ sweet red chili sauce
□ vegan worcestershire sauce
□ yellow mustard

refrigerated

□ capers
□ firm or extra-firm tofu
□ nondairy milk (e.g., rice, almond, or soy milk)

- ☐ olives
- ☐ yellow or chickpea miso

produce

- ☐ apples
- ☐ bell peppers
- ☐ blueberries
- ☐ carrots
- ☐ celery stalks
- ☐ corn
- ☐ cucumbers
- ☐ fresh ginger
- ☐ fresh herbs (parsley, thyme, basil, mint, cilantro, etc.)
- ☐ garlic cloves
- ☐ green beans
- ☐ green onions
- ☐ kale
- ☐ lemons
- ☐ limes
- ☐ mushrooms
- ☐ onions
- ☐ oranges
- ☐ peas
- ☐ potatoes
- ☐ red onions
- ☐ spinach
- ☐ sweet potatoes
- ☐ tomatoes
- ☐ zucchini

spices

- ☐ bay leaf
- ☐ cajun seasoning
- ☐ cayenne pepper
- ☐ chili powder
- ☐ chipotle powder
- ☐ dried oregano
- ☐ dried thyme
- ☐ dry mustard
- ☐ garam masala
- ☐ garlic powder (granulated)
- ☐ ground cinnamon
- ☐ ground coriander
- ☐ ground cumin
- ☐ ground ginger
- ☐ ground nutmeg
- ☐ Italian seasoning
- ☐ mild curry powder
- ☐ nutritional yeast
- ☐ onion powder (granulated)
- ☐ paprika
- ☐ pumpkin pie spice
- ☐ red pepper flakes
- ☐ smoked paprika
- ☐ turmeric

how to use icons

- ✔ **QUICK** Recipes that come together in 30 minutes or less. Some recipes may require multitasking to complete in 30 minutes.

- ✔ **FAT-FREE** Recipes with less than 1g of fat per serving.

- ✔ **GLUTEN-FREE** Recipes that don't require whole-wheat flour, vital wheat gluten, seitan, or barley. I can't vouch for all the ingredients, so if you have an allergy or sensitivity, please make sure every ingredient you use is a certified gluten-free brand. Wheat-free tamari is a good gluten-free substitute for soy sauce.

- ✔ **SOY-FREE** Recipes that don't require tofu, soy sauce, or other soy products. If the recipe calls for nondairy milk, use almond or rice milk. Also, use chickpea miso in recipes calling for miso, and coconut aminos can replace soy sauce.

- ✔ **ONE-POT MEAL** Meals that are prepared using only one pot or baking dish.

- ✔ **BUDGET** Recipes that cost roughly $5 or less to make with a well-stocked pantry and spice rack.

- ✔ **PANTRY** Recipes that can be made using only pantry ingredients, no fresh foods required. Some "pantry" recipes may list frozen foods, but the canned equivalent is also suitable.

Nothing is so beautiful as
my Compassion, my Conciousness,
my Indiviualitat, my humanity
my failures, my helblessnes
my doubts, my love
my life! — Suresh.

"Nothing is so beautiful as my compassion, my consciousness, my individuality, my humanity, my failures, my helplessness, my doubts, my love, my life!"

—Suresh (written on a chalkboard in Salzburg, Austria)

soups, stews, & chilis

GERMANY

german lentil soup

I had the most incredible lentil soup in Hamburg, Germany, and it took three tries to re-create it perfectly. I left the following note in my research book after eating it: "This lentil-carrot-potato soup was just lovely. It had an underlying hint of lemon and a touch of coriander. I can't wait to re-create it for my next book!"

SERVES 3

- 1 small onion, diced
- 2 garlic cloves, minced
- ½ tsp ground cumin
- 1½ tsp ground coriander, divided
- 2 carrots, skinned and sliced
- 1 c lentils
- 1 potato, diced
- 3 c vegetable broth, divided
- lemon zest
- parsley (garnish)

Line a medium pot with a thin layer of water (or broth) and sauté onions and garlic over high heat until onions are translucent, about 2 minutes. Add cumin and ½ tsp coriander, then stir to combine. Add carrots, plus another splash of water if necessary, and cook for a minute. Then add lentils, diced potato, and 2 c broth. Cover, bring to a boil, and simmer until lentils are softer and liquid has evaporated—about 40 minutes. Stir in remaining 1 tsp coriander and a pinch or two lemon zest. Then add up to an additional 1 c broth so it's more stew-like and not just a pot of lentils and vegetables. Add salt to taste and more coriander if desired. Garnish with parsley.

PER SERVING | Calories 315, Total Fat 0.9g, Carbohydrates 59.3g, Fiber 22.4g, Sugars 5.7g, Protein 18.5g

cuban black bean soup

CUBA

I attended high school just outside of Tampa, Florida, where Cuban cuisine is popular due to Ybor City's rich history. Ybor City was founded by cigar manufacturers in the late 1800s, and thousands of people immigrated to the area from Cuba. Cuban black bean soup was something I always longed for and missed, until I found a vegetarian version in an old issue of *Eating Well*. I've since adapted that recipe to be vegan and more reminiscent of the soup I grew up with.

Line a skillet with a thin layer of water (or vegetable broth). Sauté onion over high heat until translucent—about 2–3 minutes. Add chili powder and cumin, and stir to combine. Then add beans, vegetable broth, and salsa. Bring to a boil, then reduce to low and simmer for 10 minutes. Remove from heat and stir in lime juice. Transfer half of the mixture to a blender and puree until mostly smooth. Mix puree back in with soup. Garnish with cilantro, green onions, and broken corn chips. You can also drizzle with hot sauce or add cayenne pepper to taste, if desired.

SERVES 2

- ½ small onion, chopped
- 1½ tsp chili powder
- 1 tsp ground cumin
- 1 15-oz can black beans, drained and rinsed
- 1½ c vegetable broth
- ¼ c prepared salsa
- 1½ tsp lime juice
- 2 tbsp fresh cilantro, chopped (garnish)
- 1–2 green onions, sliced (garnish)
- corn chips, crumbled (garnish)
- hot sauce or cayenne pepper (optional)

Chef's Note You can make your own corn chips from corn tortillas. Crisp tortillas in a toaster oven or oven (350°F) for a few minutes until crisp.

PER SERVING | Calories 387, Total Fat 4.1g, Carbohydrates 69.4g, Fiber 22.7g, Sugars 5g, Protein 22.1g

FRANCE

cassoulet

■■ **PRONUNCIATION TIP**
The "t" is silent, sounds like "cas-sou-ley."

Cassoulet is a French comfort food—a rich, slow-cooked white bean stew originating from the south of France. I first came across cassoulet at the grocery store in St. Maarten (it was sitting among the canned beans), but it wasn't until I was actually in France that I came to appreciate the cultural significance of this dish. Each region has its own variation that reflects local specialties, and that tradition, I've created a vegan version. *Bon appétit!*

SERVES 3

- 8 oz vegetable broth
- 1 onion, diced
- 4 garlic cloves, minced
- 2 carrots, skinned and chopped
- 2 celery stalks, chopped
- 2 tbsp fresh thyme, divided
- 2 tbsp fresh parsley, divided
- 1 tomato, diced
- 2 tbsp tomato paste
- 1 15-oz can white beans (any kind), undrained
- thyme sprig (garnish)

Chef's Note For a more traditional experience, add sliced vegan sausage.

Chef's Note Use no-salt-added or low-sodium beans if possible.

Line a large pot with a thin layer of vegetable broth, and sauté onion and garlic over high heat until onions start to become translucent, about 2 minutes. Add carrots, celery, and remaining broth and bring to a boil. Once boiling, reduce to medium, cover, and keep cooking until carrots are softer but still firm, about 5 minutes. Add 1 tbsp fresh thyme, 1 tbsp fresh parsley, diced tomato, and tomato paste, stirring to combine. Continue to cook until carrots are fork-tender and soft, but not mushy or falling apart—about 4 more minutes. Stir in beans (with liquid) until well combined and add remaining fresh thyme and parsley. Reduce heat to low and cook until beans are warm. Ladle into a bowl and garnish with a thyme sprig.

Chef's Note This recipe is adapted from *Gourmet* (March 2008).

PER SERVING | Calories 222, Total Fat 1g, Carbohydrates 43.4g, Fiber 10.7g, Sugars 6.3g, Protein 12.7g

HUNGARY

goulash

▬▬▬ PRONUNCIATION TIP
▬▬▬ *Gulyásleves* sounds like "gool-ya-sla-vesh."

Gulyásleves (literally "goulash soup") is one of Hungary's national dishes, though you can find it all over Europe. To test the authenticity of my recipe, I had a Hungarian friend of mine try it and he said this stew would be called "New World Goulash" in Hungarian circles because it's stew-like and not cream-based (and yes, he liked it, and he's an omnivore!). Serve this stew over Polenta (pg. 121), pasta, or rice.

SERVES 4

- ¾ c vegetable broth
- 2 garlic cloves, minced
- 1 red bell pepper, seeded and diced
- 1 carrot, skinned and sliced
- 1 celery stalk, sliced
- 1 potato, diced
- ¼ tsp cayenne pepper
- 1 tsp dried thyme
- 1 tsp paprika (Hungarian, if you have it)
- 1 bay leaf
- 1 tsp red wine vinegar
- 1 tsp tomato paste
- 1 14.5-oz can diced tomatoes, undrained
- 8 oz mushrooms, stems removed
- 2–3 tbsp Vegan Worcestershire Sauce (pg. 237)

Chef's Note Goulash is traditionally made with caraway seeds; feel free to add ¼ tsp if you have them on hand.

Line a large pot with a thin layer of broth. Sauté garlic over high heat for 30 seconds, then add bell pepper, carrot, celery, and potato. Sprinkle with seasonings, add bay leaf, and bring to a boil. Sauté over high heat, stirring frequently, until potatoes are golden and liquid has evaporated. Add remaining broth, vinegar, tomato paste, tomatoes (with juice), and cover. Bring to a boil then reduce to low and simmer. Meanwhile, chop mushrooms into a sliced olive consistency and add with 2 tbsp Vegan Worcestershire Sauce. Continue to simmer until potatoes are fork-tender, stirring occasionally. Taste, adding more Vegan Worcestershire Sauce, tomato paste, or cayenne as desired. Remove bay leaf and season with salt and pepper.

PER SERVING | Calories 98, Total Fat 1g, Carbohydrates 18.9g, Fiber 4.3g, Sugars 5.6g, Protein 6.5g

SPAIN

cream of vegetables

PRONUNCIATION TIP
Crema de Verduras sounds like "crame-ah day bear-duhr-us." The "v" in Spanish sounds more like a "b."

In Spanish, this traditional dish is called *Crema de Verduras*. As the name suggests, this soup is creamy, but the creaminess comes from potatoes, not actual cream, making it accidentally vegan. Woohoo!

SERVES 2

- vegetable broth, as needed
- 1 leek, sliced
- 4 garlic cloves, minced
- 1 zucchini, cubed
- 4 carrots, sliced
- 1 potato, cubed small
- smoked paprika (garnish)

Chef's Note You can use an onion instead of a leek (leeks are more traditional in Spanish recipes) and yellow squash instead of zucchini.

Line a medium pot with a thin layer of vegetable broth, and sauté leeks and garlic over high heat until most of the liquid has evaporated, about 2 minutes. Add remaining vegetables and just enough water to cover the top of the veggies. Cover, bring to a boil, and reduce to low. Simmer until all veggies are fork-tender, about 10 to 20 minutes. Drain off (but catch) the cooking liquid and transfer vegetables to a blender with 1 c cooking liquid. Blend, adding more cooking liquid as necessary until the soup is smooth and creamy. Season generously with salt and pepper, and garnish with smoked paprika.

PER SERVING

Calories 168, Total Fat 0.7g, Carbohydrates 38.4g, Fiber 7.3g, Sugars 10.0g, Protein 5.1g

taco soup

MEXICO

All the flavors of a taco turned into a filling soup! I first came across taco soup while living in Los Angeles, California (SoCal cuisine has a heavy Mexican influence). I'm pretty sure this dish is an American creation, though it's clearly inspired by Mexican cuisine. I took care to celebrate the flavors of Mexico in my interpretation of this recipe, which creates an authentic taste and ethnic experience.

Combine all ingredients together in a medium pot, stirring to combine. Cover and cook over low heat until thoroughly warm, about 15–20 minutes. (The slower cooking time helps bring out the flavors.) Once warm, season with salt and pepper to taste, ladle into soup bowls, and garnish with optional toppings.

Chef's Note You can add more green chilies to this soup for a spicier taste.

PER SERVING	Calories 501, Total Fat 5.5g, Carbohydrates 92.6g, Fiber 30.5g, Sugars 14.7g, Protein 30.2g

SERVES 2

- 1 14-oz can diced tomatoes, with juices
- 1 c vegetable broth
- 1 15-oz can black beans, drained and rinsed
- 1 c frozen corn
- ¼ c salsa
- 2 tbsp nutritional yeast
- 2 tbsp green chilies, minced
- 1 tbsp chili powder
- 1½ tsp ground cumin
- 1 tsp dried oregano or marjoram
- 1 tsp onion powder (granulated)
- 1 tsp garlic powder (granulated)
- ½ tsp paprika
- ⅛ tsp cayenne pepper (optional)

OPTIONAL TOPPINGS

- corn chips, crumbled
- cilantro
- Sour Cream (pg. 239) or vegan plain yogurt
- hot sauce

SWEDEN

swedish split pea soup

Split pea soups are popular in several cuisines and cultures: Britain, Ireland, Canada, Germany, the Netherlands, Finland, Sweden, and America, just to name a few. This split pea soup is a vegan version of Swedish split pea soup (called *ärtsoppa* in Swedish), which rose to popularity in the 16th century as a Thursday dinner due to Catholic influence and fasting on Fridays. Despite a different religious climate in Sweden today, this soup remains a popular Thursday dinner dish.

SERVES 2

- 3 c vegetable broth, divided
- ½ onion, diced
- 2 carrots, sliced
- 1 c yellow split peas
- 1 tsp tomato paste
- ½ tsp smoked paprika
- ¼ tsp pure maple syrup

Chef's Note This soup is traditionally made with ham. I find the smoked paprika and pure maple syrup capture that flavor essence perfectly.

Line a skillet with a thin layer of broth and sauté onions and carrots over high heat until onions are translucent and carrots are fork-tender, about 2–3 minutes. Transfer onions and carrots to a blender and blend with 2 c broth until well combined. Return to pot and add peas. Bring to a boil, cover, and reduce to low. Simmer for 30 minutes or until water has been absorbed and peas are soft but not mushy. If they are still pretty hard after 30 minutes, add remaining broth and continue to cook. They should be soft, not hard—but not mushy and falling apart. Once peas are cooked, add 1–4 tbsp water or broth so the mixture is a little wet but not soupy. Stir in tomato paste, paprika, and maple syrup.

PER SERVING | Calories 400, Total Fat 1.4g, Carbohydrates 75.2g, Fiber 27.6g, Sugars 14.3g, Protein 25.2g

quick chili mole

MEXICO

PRONUNCIATION TIP
Mole in Spanish sounds like "mo-lay."

I discovered Mexican mole sauce far too late in life. For that reason, I'm trying to pull the key flavors together in all sorts of fusion dishes—like this quick and easy chili! To extend this dish, add canned pinto beans (drained and rinsed) and/or corn.

SERVES 3

- 1 c vegetable broth
- 1 small onion, diced
- 4 garlic cloves, minced
- 1 c refried beans
- ½ tsp ground cumin
- ¼ tsp chipotle powder
- 4 tsp unsweetened cocoa
- 1 14-oz can diced tomatoes, undrained
- green onions (optional)
- lime wedges (garnish)

Sauté onions and garlic in a thin layer of broth over high heat until onions are translucent, about 2–3 minutes. Reduce to medium heat and add remaining broth, refried beans, cumin, chipotle powder, cocoa, and tomatoes with their juices, stirring to combine. Reduce heat to low and warm thoroughly, about 5–7 minutes. Once warm, taste, adding more chipotle powder if you want more heat (be careful—a little goes a long way!). You can also add more cocoa, if desired, but too much cocoa can leave a chalky taste. If you choose to add more chipotle powder or cocoa, add each in ¼-tsp increments. Garnish with sliced green onions and a lime wedge, if desired. If you go spicy with extra chipotle, plain vegan yogurt or Sour Cream (pg. 239) makes a nice garnish.

Chef's Note Mole sauce is the generic term for a number of different sauces in Mexican cuisine, but outside of Mexico, "mole sauce" typically refers to mole poblano, a dark, rich sauce containing cocoa (though the sauce itself isn't chocolaty). See my recipe for Quick Mole Sauce (pg. 207).

PER SERVING | Calories 134, Total Fat 1.5g, Carbohydrates 26.1g, Fiber 8g, Sugars 6.1g, Protein 6.8g

thai noodle soup

THAILAND

If you like America's chicken noodle soup, you'll love this Thai cousin! Noodle soups are a staple in several Asian countries: Cambodia, China, Japan, Korea, Indonesia, Thailand, and Vietnam, for example. In Thailand specifically, noodle soups are a popular street cart food and fast food.

Remove rooty bottoms from green onions and mince white and light green parts, slicing dark green parts and setting them aside. In a saucepan, combine water, bouillon cube, fresh ginger, and minced green onions and bring to a boil. Once boiling, add noodles and cook 2 minutes, or until they are done (they cook fast!). Turn off heat and add soy sauce, chili sauce, miso, sliced dark green parts of the onions, basil, and cilantro, stirring to combine. Taste, adding more soy sauce and ground ginger if desired (I like mine really gingery, so I add about 1 tsp). Sprinkle red pepper flakes on top and serve.

Chef's Note White or red miso may be substituted in this recipe. Do not use brown miso.

Chef's Note You can find vermicelli or maifun noodles in the Asian section of your local grocery store (check the bottom shelves). These noodles are super thin—thinner than spaghetti. I usually buy Annie Chun's maifun noodles, which are made from brown rice.

SERVES 2

- 3 green onions
- 4 c water
- 1 vegetable bouillon cube
- 2 tbsp fresh ginger, minced
- 2 oz vermicelli or maifun noodles
- 2 tbsp low-sodium soy sauce
- 3 tbsp sweet red chili sauce
- 1 tsp yellow miso
- ¼ c fresh basil
- ¼ c fresh cilantro
- ground ginger (optional)
- red pepper flakes (garnish)

Chef's Note You can substitute 2 c vegetable broth for 2 c water and bouillon cube.

PER SERVING | Calories 192, Total Fat 0.8g, Carbohydrates 42.3g, Fiber 2.2g, Sugars 11.2g, Protein 3.8g

SPAIN

gazpacho

Gazpacho originates from Andalusia, my favorite part of Spain, and it's traditionally vegan. The first time I ever had gazpacho was actually in Andalusia, back in 2007. Scott and I had just arrived in *Sevilla* (pronounced like "sa-vee-ya") and dipped into the first café we saw, hoping to find a quick bite to eat. It was fairly late in the afternoon, just after siesta, and the restaurant wasn't yet serving its dinner menu (Spaniards eat dinner rather late at night by American standards—after 9:00 p.m.), but the waiter offered to bring us two bowls of gazpacho left over from lunch. The idea of a cold soup initially sounded strange to me, but I was so hungry and melting under the fierce Andalusian sun that I was willing to try anything that was cool and nourishing. After a few spoonfuls, I felt ashamed for being so pessimistic—gazpacho is deliciously light and refreshing!

SERVES 2

- 1 slice stale or toasted bread
- 3 plum tomatoes
- 6" cucumber
- 1–2 garlic cloves
- 1 red bell pepper, seeded
- 2–3 green onions
- hot sauce (optional)
- red wine vinegar (optional)

Chef's Note For a cool and refreshing soup, store your veggies in the fridge before use. You can also add an ice cube to the mix, if necessary.

Chef's Note The heel of the bread is best in this recipe. Finally, a use for the heel!

Chef's Note If you don't have a strong enough blender, you may need to chop your vegetables up before-hand.

Combine all ingredients in a blender and pulverize into a soup, adding ice-cold water as necessary to achieve the right smoothness and soup consistency. Taste, adding hot sauce or red wine vinegar if desired. Top with chopped raw veggies, like Spanish onions, bell peppers, or celery.

PER SERVING Calories 118, Total Fat 1.2g, Carbohydrates 24.1g, Fiber 5.3g, Sugars 12.5g, Protein 5.7g

Munich, Germany (2011)

bavarian onion soup

GERMANY

PRONUNCIATION TIP
Zwiebel ("zwee-bul") is the German word for onion, and *suppe* ("zoo-puh") is the German word for soup, hence *zwiebelsuppe* ("zwee-bulz-a-puh") literally means "onion soup." *Bayerische* ("Bavarian") sounds like "Bi-yer-ish-shay."

This German soup (called *Bayerische Zwiebelsuppe* in German) is the cousin to French onion soup—except it uses beer and doesn't have cheese or bread in it (though it's delightful served with rye bread for dipping).

Prepare bouquet: Place peppercorns, garlic, and all herbs/spices in a piece of cheesecloth and tie into a small bag. If you don't have cheesecloth, you can try using a coffee filter tied off at the end. Set aside.

Cut onion in half, then slice thinly so you get long, thin onion pieces. Line medium pot with water and sauté onions over high heat until they are softer and translucent. Then add broth and bouquet. Bring to a boil, reduce to low, and simmer for 30 minutes. Pour in beer and stir to combine. Remove bouquet and discard. Add salt and pepper to taste, if necessary.

SERVES 2

- 2 tbsp black peppercorns
- 1 large garlic clove
- 1 tbsp Italian seasoning
- 1½ tsp fennel seeds
- ½ tsp nutmeg
- 1 bay leaf
- 1 large sweet onion
- 3 c No-Beef Broth (pg. 234)
- 1 c beer (pilsner)

Chef's Note Avoid using a bitter beer here, or your soup may end up bitter.

PER SERVING | Calories 153, Total Fat 2.9g, Carbohydrates 22g, Fiber 4.2g, Sugars 5.1g, Protein 4.2g

Seville, Spain (2006)

The first time I traveled to Europe, I went to find myself. I know how cliché that sounds, but I was at a crossroads in my life and hoped that some time away, time to reflect . . . would help guide me to a decision. I had just completed my first two years of law school and had another year left. Although I had wanted to go to law school so badly, I found myself feeling listless and not wanting to stay. I hadn't enjoyed my classes or my work, and I couldn't shake this nagging feeling that I was being pulled farther away from where I really wanted to go.

Cinque Terre, Italy (2006)

A part of me wanted to quit and find a more suitable path to travel down, but another part of me couldn't bear the thought of quitting. I had just spent two years and thousands of dollars to pursue this career and education; I might as well finish it. There was also the looming pressure of pride and the anxiety of letting others down. It didn't help that I had no idea what I wanted to do or what I would pursue if I walked away from the law.

Four weeks later, I still had not found the answers for which I was so desperately searching. I still felt lost. I still had that nagging feeling I was heading in the wrong direction and I still had all the pressure, fear,

Prague (Praha), Czech Republic (2006)

Wachua Valley, Austria (2006)

Barcelona, Spain (2011)

and anxiety crippling me. I went back to law school and finished—and then I left the law for good two years later.

In Barcelona, more than five years after my first soul-searching trip to Europe, I met Benjamin. He was standing in line at the train station and asked the crowd if anyone spoke English and Spanish. I offered to help and after his travel was squared away, we chatted briefly. (A true testament that veg-heads attract each other, by the way. Benjamin was a vegetarian from Budapest!) Benjamin happened to be passing through Barcelona on his way to *El Camino de Santiago*, a pilgrimage route through northern Spain. I asked Benjamin if he was soul searching (as I had been so many years ago), and he replied, "No, I'm letting my soul find me." And in that moment, Benjamin changed my life.

legume-based dishes

lentil taco "meat"

MEXICO

Clearly, I'm destined to have a taco recipe in every cookbook I write. That's okay though, because I love tacos and this Lentil Taco "Meat" is my favorite taco filling yet! I got this idea from one of my fans and now we make lentil tacos (or burritos, or enchiladas!) at least once a week. Use brown- or the greenish-colored lentils here, not red or yellow.

Pulse warm lentils in a food processor or blender until chopped up or pureed (your choice). Transfer to a mixing bowl and stir in remaining ingredients. Taste, adding salt or pepper as desired, plus a splash of nondairy milk or a touch of salsa if the mixture looks dry.

Chef's Note If you can find canned (already cooked) lentils, you can substitute them here, though be mindful that you may want to reduce or eliminate the soy sauce, especially if your lentils are not low-sodium/salt-free.

PER SERVING | Calories 137, Total Fat 1.1g, Carbohydrates 23.9g, Fiber 9g, Sugars 3.9g, Protein 9.9g

SERVES 4

- 2 c cooked lentils
- 2 tbsp ketchup
- 1 tbsp prepared yellow mustard
- 1 tbsp low-sodium soy sauce
- 1 tbsp chili powder
- 2 tsp lemon or lime (juice)
- 1½ tsp ground cumin
- ½ tsp paprika
- ¼ tsp garlic powder (granulated)
- ¼ tsp onion powder (granulated)
- ¼ tsp dried oregano or marjoram
- ⅛ tsp cayenne pepper (optional)
- nondairy milk (optional)
- salsa (optional)

Chef's Note For a gluten-free option, use wheat-free tamari instead of soy sauce.

GERMANY

spicy mustard chickpeas

SERVES 2

- vegetable broth, as needed
- 1 tbsp and 1 tsp hot sauce, divided
- 1 tbsp and 1 tsp yellow mustard, divided
- 1 tbsp low-sodium soy sauce
- ½ tsp garlic powder (granulated)
- ½ tsp onion powder (granulated)
- 1 tsp brown sugar (optional)
- 1 15-oz can chickpeas, drained and rinsed

Chef's Note For a gluten-free option, use wheat-free tamari instead of soy sauce.

The first time I backpacked through Europe, I came home with a vinegar obsession, particularly with balsamic vinegar. After my second backpacking trip, I came back addicted to mustard. I love all types of mustard but am especially hot for German mustard and Dijon (French) mustard. These chickpeas arose from my mustard obsession and yes, I have balsamic chickpeas in this book too (Lemon-Balsamic Chickpeas, pg. 48)!

Line a skillet with a thin layer of vegetable broth. Whisk in hot sauce, mustard, soy sauce, spices, and sugar, if using. Add chickpeas and bring to a boil. Once boiling, reduce to medium-high and continue to cook, stirring constantly, until all the liquid absorbs and the chickpeas are well coated. Add a few more drops of hot sauce (½ to 1 tsp) and a little more mustard (about 1 tsp) and stir to coat chickpeas. Serve over cooked grains or greens.

PER SERVING | Calories 224, Total Fat 1.9g, Carbohydrates 36.6g, Fiber 8.1g, Sugars 2.3g, Protein 11.9g

chickpea cacciatore

ITALY

Cacciatore literally translates to "hunter" but also refers to any meat dish prepared with tomatoes, onions, fresh herbs, and Italian wine. (In northern Italy, cacciatore is prepared with white wine and in southern Italy, red wine is used.) Here I'm using chickpeas so it would be called *Ceci alla Cacciatora*.

Pour juice from canned tomatoes into a skillet. Add water or vegetable broth as necessary to achieve a thin layer of liquid. Add onions and garlic, if using, and sauté over high heat until onions are translucent, about 2 minutes. Turn off heat, adding more liquid so you have a thin layer again. Pull tomatoes apart with your fingers (careful—they squirt liquid!) into bite-sized pieces and place them in the skillet. Add mushrooms and 1 tsp Italian seasoning and stir to combine. Sauté over high heat (cover if necessary to prevent splashing) and continue to cook until mushrooms are soft and light brown. Add wine and another 1 tsp Italian seasoning, uncover, and cook until liquid reduces by half, about 3 minutes. Just before it's done, add capers and remaining ½ tsp Italian seasoning, stirring to combine. Season with salt and black pepper, then stir in chickpeas and serve.

SERVES 2

- 1 14-oz can peeled tomatoes, with juices
- vegetable broth, as needed
- ½ onion, diced
- 3 garlic cloves, minced (optional)
- 1 c white mushrooms, sliced thin
- 2½ tsp Italian seasoning, divided
- ½ c dry wine
- 1–2 tbsp capers
- 1 15-oz can chickpeas, drained and rinsed

Chef's Note If you only have a 28-oz can of tomatoes, pull out 7–8 tomatoes plus about ½ c juice from the can for this recipe.

Chef's Note Cacciatore is not traditionally made with garlic, which is why it's listed as optional. I love the added taste of garlic in this dish, however.

PER SERVING | Calories 330, Total Fat 5.3g, Carbohydrates 46.2g, Fiber 11.6g, Sugars 9.7g, Protein 14.0g

INDIA

masoor dal

Masoor dal means "red lentils." I know, I got really creative with this dish's name! I originally called it Bengal Lentils because I got the idea for this recipe after I happened upon a dish by Tasty Bite with the same name. However, after a little research, I decided this dish didn't really reflect Bengali or, more specifically, West Bengal cuisine, so "red lentils" it is. Name drama aside, this dish is awesome!

SERVES 2

- vegetable broth, as needed
- ½ onion, diced
- 5 garlic cloves, minced
- 1 tbsp fresh ginger, minced
- red pepper flakes
- 1 tsp ground coriander
- 1 c tomato sauce
- ½ c red lentils
- 2 tsp yellow mustard
- 1 tsp garam masala
- smoked paprika

Line a medium pot with a thin layer of water or broth. Sauté onion, garlic, ginger, and red pepper flakes over high heat until onions are translucent—about a minute. Stir in coriander so that the onions, garlic, and ginger are well coated. Add tomato sauce and stir, then add red lentils and 1 c water. Cover, bring to a boil, then reduce to low and simmer. Continue to cook until the lentils are soft and mushy (they will change to an orange color) and most of the liquid has absorbed—about 20 minutes. Add mustard, garam masala, and a dash or two smoked paprika, stirring to combine. Turn off heat and let rest 5–15 minutes (the longer the better). Taste, adding salt or more paprika if desired.

PER SERVING
(WITHOUT BROTH)

Calories 245, Total Fat 1.0g, Carbohydrates 46.2g, Fiber 17.8g, Sugars 8.3g, Protein 15.6g

ITALY

lemon-balsamic chickpeas

SERVES 2

- 1 15-oz can chickpeas, drained and rinsed
- ¼ c balsamic vinegar
- 1 tbsp ketchup
- ¼ tsp garlic powder (granulated)
- lemon zest
- lemon wedges
- fresh parsley, chopped (optional)

Chef's Note I find these chickpeas get more flavorful after they sit for 10–15 minutes.

Oh my goodness. I love balsamic vinegar. I'm slightly embarrassed to discuss my love affair with balsamic vinegar. I really don't know what happened. I never really cared for vinegar, but then I went to Europe and came home fixated on it. Truthfully, I'd probably take swigs from the balsamic vinegar bottle if I didn't think my family would judge me. Anyway, I love it. It's ridiculous—but in all the right ways. The sweet tanginess of balsamic goes so well with chickpeas. And the fresh lemon? It just pulls it all together to give you this flavorful but effortless Mediterranean dish. Make this dish and become obsessed like me!

Add all ingredients except lemon and parsley to a skillet and turn heat on medium-high. Sauté, stirring chickpeas constantly, until balsamic vinegar has evaporated and chickpeas are dark and caramelized. Add a pinch or two of lemon zest (the zest from half of a small lemon, or thereabouts) and serve with a lemon wedge or two. (Squeeze fresh lemon juice over the chickpeas just before eating.) Serve on a bed of greens or cooked grains such as quinoa, rice, or couscous.

PER SERVING | Calories 208, Total Fat 3.4g, Carbohydrates 32.5g, Fiber 8.9g, Sugars 3.7g, Protein 10.7g

drunken beans

MEXICO

PRONUNCIATION TIP
Frijoles borrachos sounds "free-hole-les bore-ra-chos," but remember to roll your tongue with the double r.

Frijoles borrachos (drunken beans) are a Mexican comfort food. Traditionally, the recipe involves soaking pinto beans overnight (sometimes in beer) and cooking them slowly on the stovetop for an hour or more. I've skirted most of that process with this recipe, but you still get the same flavorful drunken beans in the end. For a complete meal, serve with a side of rice and a crisp salad or AJ's Pico de Gallo (pg. 202).

Line a skillet with vegetable broth. Add jalapeño, onion, garlic, chili powder, cumin, oregano, and tomato paste and sauté over high heat until onion is translucent—about 1 minute. Turn off heat and add pinto beans. Using a fork or potato masher, mash about half of the beans. You want a good bit pureed and refried bean–like but still some whole beans left. Turn heat back on to low and add ½ c beer. Stir to combine—as it cooks, the mixture will thicken up a bit. Add salt to taste, plus smoked paprika. If it gets too thick (it should be slightly wet but not overly runny or soupy), add another ¼ c beer and cook for a few minutes to cook off some of the beer taste. Garnish with cilantro and serve with a lime wedge.

SERVES 2

- vegetable broth, as needed
- 1–2 tbsp diced jalapeño
- 1 small onion, diced
- 3 garlic cloves, minced
- 1 tsp chili powder
- 1½ tsp ground cumin
- ½ tsp dried oregano
- 2 tbsp tomato paste
- 1 15-oz can pinto beans, drained and rinsed
- ½–¾ c beer (e.g., Corona)
- ¼ tsp smoked paprika
- cilantro (garnish)
- lime wedge (garnish)

Chef's Note I use canned minced jalapeños when I make this recipe. You may need to adjust if you use fresh.

PER SERVING | Calories 230, Total Fat 2.5g, Carbohydrates 37.2g, Fiber 10.6g, Sugars 5.6g, Protein 12.1g

nona's chickpeas

PORTUGAL

One of my favorite parts of traveling is the actual traveling—sitting on a train, bus, or plane. I always meet the most fascinating people, and my trip from Madrid to Granada was no exception. I became chatty with the woman sitting next to me, and after she realized I was American, she asked what I was doing in Spain. I explained that I was traveling through Europe researching for my next cookbook—that's when she immediately summoned her mother in a neighboring row. We communicated through drawings, various hand gestures, and with the help of my Spanish–English dictionary. Of all the recipes they shared with me that day, this was my favorite because Nona only told me the ingredients, saying the method was as simple as cooking with my heart—*"Cocinar con el corazón."*

SERVES 2

- vegetable broth, as needed
- 5 garlic cloves, minced
- 1 red bell pepper, seeded and diced
- ¼ c green olives, sliced
- 3 tbsp raisins, finely chopped
- 1 15-oz can chickpeas, drained and rinsed
- smoked paprika
- ¼ c fresh parsley, finely chopped

Line a skillet with a thin layer of broth, and sauté garlic and bell pepper over high heat until garlic is golden, bell pepper is soft, and the liquid has evaporated or is mostly evaporated. Add olives and continue to cook, adding a bit more broth if necessary, until olives are fragrant, about 20–30 seconds. Add raisins and continue to cook until they soften up a bit, about 1 minute. Stir in chickpeas, then add a few dashes of smoked paprika. Stir in parsley, and taste, adding more paprika if desired. Serve warm or cold over a bed of baby spinach or couscous.

PER SERVING

Calories 281, Total Fat 4.8g, Carbohydrates 47.7g, Fiber 10.7g, Sugars 12.4g, Protein 12.4g

GERMANY

german sandwich spread

SERVES 4 (MAKES 1 CUP)

- 1 c canned white beans, drained and rinsed
- 1 red bell pepper, seeded and sliced
- 1 tsp chili powder
- 1 tsp onion flakes
- 3–4 tbsp nutritional yeast
- smoked paprika
- cayenne pepper
- ¼ c cooked potato, chopped or mashed (optional)

Chef's Note For a thicker spread, add ¼ c cooked potato. (I recommend mashing or chopping it, not adding it whole to your food processor or blender.)

Chef's Note Add 1 tbsp ketchup if you'd like a tomato variation.

A wonderful Herbie put me up when I was in Hamburg. After a late night of festivities (read: beer drinking), I woke up the next morning to a beautiful breakfast spread. What intrigued me the most was this little can sitting next to the fresh bread. I was scoping it out when my host told me it was a sandwich spread. I was a little skeptical about a spread that went on bread and lived in a can . . . and then I tried it. I liked it so much that I made my host take me to a store where I proceeded to buy six more cans. I still dream about those spreads in Germany, but this at-home version is pretty close!

Combine beans, bell pepper, chili powder, onion flakes, 3 tbsp nutritional yeast, a pinch of salt, a few dashes of smoked paprika, potato (if desired), and as much cayenne as you want in a blender or food processor and whiz until smooth and creamy, stopping to scrape sides as necessary until you reach a thick, hummus-like consistency. Taste, adding more nutritional yeast or salt if desired. Smear on rustic bread or crackers.

PER SERVING

Calories 80, Total Fat 0.6g, Carbohydrates 15.0g, Fiber 6.3g, Sugars 1.5g, Protein 6.8g

WITH KETCHUP
Calories 83, Total Fat 0.6g, Carbohydrates 15.9g, Fiber 6.3g, Sugars 2.3g, Protein 6.9g

taquitos

MEXICO

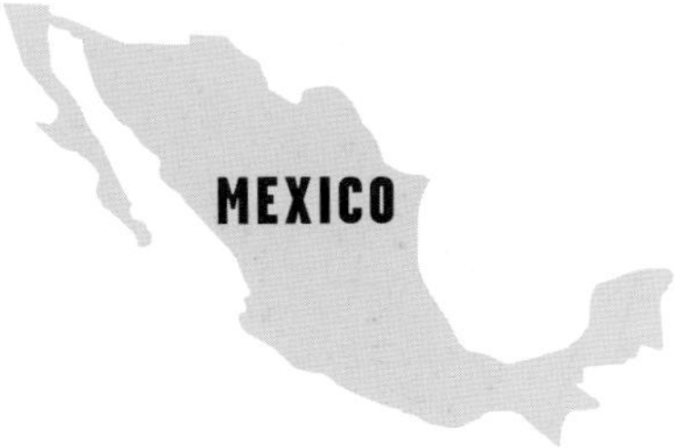

Taquitos are tightly rolled, deep-fried tortillas that look like cigars. Although they were invented in California, taquitos are considered a Mexican food. Taquitos in Mexico are called *tacos dorados*, which means "golden tacos," or *flautas*, which translates to "flutes." Taquitos are traditionally served with salsa and guacamole.

SERVES 8

1 15-oz can refried beans

8 whole-wheat flour tortillas

Preheat oven to 350°F. Line a cookie sheet with parchment paper and set aside. Spread a thin layer of refried beans (about ¼ c) on each tortilla. Roll up into a cigar shape (much thinner than a burrito). Place crease-side down and bake 5 minutes. Flip and bake again for another 5 minutes, repeating as necessary until golden and crispy but not burned. Taquitos usually take about 15 minutes total, but cooking time can vary based on your oven, the type of tortillas used, and the size of your taquitos. Serve with salsa, Sour Cream (pg. 239), or guacamole for dipping.

PER SERVING
(1 TORTILLA, ¼ CUP REFRIED BEANS)

Calories 89, Total Fat 0.7g, Carbohydrates 17.3g, Fiber 4.0g, Sugars 0g, Protein 3.8g

MEXICO

migas

PRONUNCIATION TIP
Migas sounds like "mee-gas."

If you love tofu scramble, you will love this vegan take on Tex-Mex migas. Traditionally, migas consist of scrambled eggs (or here, scrambled tofu) mixed with strips of corn tortillas and served with salsa, plus a side of warmed, re-fried beans.

SERVES 2

- 2 corn tortillas
- 3 green onions
- 1 poblano pepper, seeded and diced (optional)
- 1 lb firm or extra firm tofu, crumbled
- 1 tsp onion powder (granulated)
- 1 tsp garlic powder (granulated)
- ¾ tsp ground cumin
- turmeric
- 1 tbsp Dijon mustard
- nondairy milk
- ¼ c cilantro
- salsa (topping)
- refried beans

Preheat oven to 350°F. Place corn tortillas on rack and bake 5–10 minutes, until crisp. Slice tortillas into 1-inch strips (cutting longest pieces in half). Cut bottoms off green onions and mince white and light green parts, reserving dark green parts for later. Line a skillet with a thin layer of water and sauté minced white and light green parts of onion plus poblano pepper over high heat until the liquid has absorbed. Add tofu, tortilla pieces, onion powder, garlic powder, cumin, a few dashes of turmeric, and Dijon mustard, continuing to cook and stirring constantly. Add splashes of nondairy milk as necessary to prevent sticking and to slightly soften the tortilla pieces. When tofu is warm, stir in cilantro and remaining dark green parts of onion. Stir to combine the mixture thoroughly. Add salt and pepper to taste.

PER SERVING
(WITH POBLANO)

Calories 246, Total Fat 10.8g, Carbohydrates 21.3g, Fiber 5.1g, Sugars 4.1g, Protein 21.7g

PER SERVING

Calories 237, Total Fat 10.7g, Carbohydrates 19.1g, Fiber 4.8g, Sugars 3.0g, Protein 21.3g

Innsbruck, Austria (2011)

Munich (München), Germany (2011)

When I travel in Europe, I stay in hostels. Hostels have a vibrant, social energy that you can't find anywhere else. I feel very privileged to have met people from all over the world in hostels—Chile, Japan, Australia, Canada, Argentina, Korea, India, Brazil, South Africa, New Zealand, and Egypt (just to name a few!). And I don't know where else I could have had that opportunity. I have also met people from my own country, but from states or cities I have never traveled to and may never see for myself. I love embracing moments when my path is crossing with someone I may have never otherwise met and basking in that moment of connectedness. We are two travelers on our own journeys whose paths cross, if only for a moment, and my hope is that, in meeting, we will both be forever changed.

vegetable sides

IRELAND

colcannon

PRONUNCIATION TIP
Colcannon sounds like "coal-cannon" (pronounced like the name Shannon).

SERVES 6

4 c baking potatoes, chopped

4 c cabbage or kale, chopped

nondairy milk

1 tbsp Dijon mustard

4 green onions, sliced

fresh parsley (optional garnish)

Chef's Note *Boerenkool* (which means "kale" in Dutch) is a traditional dish of mashed potatoes mixed with kale, then served with brown gravy, smoked sausage, bacon bits, and chopped pickles on the side. I use leftover Colcannon, plus Spicy Sausage, Brown Gravy, and Bacon Bits (pg. 246) recipes from *The Happy Herbivore Cookbook* to replicate it.

PRONUNCIATION TIP
Boerenkool sounds like "Boo-ren-kool."

I first came across colcannon in an Irish pub in England. It's a traditional Irish dish, and upon reading the menu description, "mashed potatoes with cabbage," I was intrigued. Who knew cabbage makes mashed potatoes?!

Bring a large pot of water to a boil, add potatoes, and boil potatoes until fork-tender, about 5 minutes. Meanwhile, line another pot with a thin layer of water and steam cabbage or kale until softer and cooked, about 1–2 minutes, then drain. When potatoes are done, drain and return to pot. Mash with a potato masher or electric beaters, adding splashes of nondairy milk as necessary to achieve the right mashed potato consistency. Add a squirt of Dijon mustard (about 1 tbsp) and mix into potatoes. Taste, adding more Dijon if desired. Add salt and pepper to taste, then stir in kale or cabbage and green onions, mixing until well combined. Garnish with chopped or minced parsley.

PER SERVING

KALE Calories 67, Total Fat 0.6g, Carbohydrates 14.2g, Fiber 2.4g, Sugars 0.6g, Protein 2.8g

CABBAGE Calories 57, Total Fat 0.4g, Carbohydrates 12.4g, Fiber 2.7g, Sugars 2.1g, Protein 1.9g

INDIA

saag

Saag is a simple but delicious Punjab dish usually made with spinach, although other greens, such as mustard greens, are sometimes used. Traditionally, *saag* is eaten with Indian breads like roti or naan, but it can also be served with rice.

SERVES 1

vegetable broth,
as needed

1 small onion, diced

3 garlic cloves, minced

1 tsp fresh ginger,
minced

2 tsp ground coriander,
divided

10 oz fresh spinach

½–1 tsp garam masala

cayenne pepper,
to taste

Line a large pot with a thin layer of broth. Sauté onion, garlic, and ginger over high heat until onion is translucent—about 2 minutes. Add 1 tsp coriander, stirring to coat, then add spinach, using tongs or a wooden spoon to constantly stir and incorporate, so spinach cooks down, is dark green and softer but not totally wilty and mushy. Add a tiny bit more broth if needed to prevent sticking, but you don't want to add too much.

Drain off excess liquid (if any) and transfer spinach mixture to a blender or food processor. Add another 1 tsp coriander and ½ tsp garam masala, plus cayenne pepper as desired. Pulse a few times so that the mixture is creamed but not mushy or pureed. Taste, adding salt as necessary, plus more garam masala or cayenne, if desired.

PER SERVING | Calories 114, Total Fat 1.4g, Carbohydrates 21.2g, Fiber 7.9g, Sugars 4.3g, Protein 9.7g

german potato salad

GERMANY

If you are unfamiliar with German potato salad, it is fairly different from mayo-heavy "American" potato salad. It is vinegar-based and served warm rather than chilled.

Steam or boil potatoes until just fork-tender. Meanwhile, line a skillet with a thin layer of water and cook onions until soft and translucent. Once onions are cooked, sprinkle dry mustard over top, stirring to incorporate, and set aside. Whisk vinegar, water, agave nectar, flour, Dijon mustard, and a dash of nutritional yeast together in a measuring cup. Add ½ to 1 tsp salt and black pepper (or to taste) and set aside. You can also add a little more agave if you don't want a strong vinegar flavor. Once potatoes are cooked, run under cool water for a few seconds so they are safe to handle, but still warm. Gently remove skins. Cube potatoes— you should have approximately 3 c cubed potatoes. In a mixing bowl, toss potatoes with onion mixture. Re-whisk vinegar mixture, and pour over potatoes, stirring to combine. Add most of the Bacon Bits, reserving about 1 tbsp to sprinkle over top, and mix again. Let the mixture rest for 10–20 minutes, if possible. Then, gently mix in chopped green onions. Transfer to a serving bowl and garnish with remaining Bacon Bits and more green onions. Serve warm.

SERVES 4

- 3 small brown potatoes
- 1 onion, diced
- ¼ tsp dry mustard (spice, not condiment)
- ¼ c white vinegar
- 2 tbsp water
- 1¼ tbsp agave nectar
- 1 tbsp whole-wheat pastry flour
- 1 tsp Dijon mustard
  nutritional yeast
- ⅛ tsp black pepper
- ½ tsp salt
- ¼ c Bacon Bits (pg. 246)
- 1 bunch green onions, chopped

Chef's Note Although I hate to admit it, all-purpose flour works best in this recipe.

Chef's Note I use Bacon Bits (pg. 246) here, but any brand of commercial bacon bits (most are vegan!) can be substituted.

PER SERVING | Calories 133, Total Fat 0.3g, Carbohydrates 29.2g, Fiber 4.6g, Sugars 3.1g, Protein 3.3g

IRELAND

champ

Champ is a classic Irish side dish. If you love traditional mashed potatoes, you're in for a treat with this Irish cousin.

SERVES 3

- 3 medium brown potatoes
- 1 bunch green onions, sliced
- ½ c nondairy milk
- onion powder (granulated) (optional)

Chef's Note If you want to use electric beaters, drain the liquid off the onions into the potatoes (reserving the cooked onions) and beat. Once potatoes are whipped and mashed, stir in green onions. (You don't want to use the beaters on the green onions, you want them to remain whole and lightly mixed in to the mashed potatoes.)

Bring a large pot of water to a boil. Cube potatoes and boil until fork-tender. Once potatoes are cooked, strain in a colander and return potatoes to the pot and cover. Meanwhile, sauté green onions in nondairy milk until just soft and milk starts to bubble from boiling. Mash potatoes with a potato masher, then add milk–onion mixture. Continue to mash until you have mashed potatoes. At first it will appear too soupy—it's not. Keep mashing, and stir periodically to combine. Season generously with salt and pepper. You can also add a little onion powder if you want a stronger onion flavoring.

PER SERVING | Calories 170, Total Fat 0.8g, Carbohydrates 37.5g, Fiber 6.6g, Sugars 3.6g, Protein 4.7g

mediterranean chard

SPAIN

GREECE

ITALY

You know what I love about Mediterranean cuisine? Olives. Olives are one of the few foods I feast on when I travel, and every time I eat them fresh in the Mediterranean, I fall a little more in love. This dish celebrates the olive! For a full meal, add chickpeas.

Line skillet with a thin layer of vegetable broth, and sauté garlic and a pinch of red pepper flakes over high heat for a minute or two, until the garlic is golden in color, fragrant, and most of the broth has cooked off. Add enough broth to line the skillet again, then add capers and olives. Sauté for a few seconds, then add greens. Stir to combine and continue to cook, using tongs or a spatula to stir the greens around, incorporating them with the other ingredients and to help cook them down. Once greens are dark in color and softer, about 2–3 minutes, turn off heat. Add lemon zest and stir to combine before serving.

SERVES 2

vegetable broth, as needed

8 garlic cloves, minced

red pepper flakes

2 tsp capers

⅓ c olives, sliced thin

2–3 c chard, chopped

1 tsp lemon (zest)

Chef's Note Feel free to scale back the garlic, particularly if you have bigger cloves. I love the strong taste of garlic in this dish, but if you're not a garlic lover, 8 cloves might be overpowering.

Chef's Note While any olive will do here, kalamata olives are best.

PER SERVING
(WITH 3 CUPS CHARD)

Calories 57, Total Fat 2.6g, Carbohydrates 8.3g, Fiber 2g, Sugar 0.3g, Protein 2g

SPAIN

patatas bravas

Patatas bravas is a popular tapas in Spain. (The term "tapas" refers to a wide variety of appetizers or snacks in Spanish cuisine.) In Spain, dinner is served late (after 9:00 p.m.), so Spaniards tend to socialize before dinner, while sharing tapas. Additionally, in some cities, such as Madrid and Granada, if you order a drink at the bar, a tapa is complimentary!

SERVES 4

2 potatoes, cubed

SAUCE
1½ tbsp tomato paste
1 large tomato
¼ c white wine
1 tbsp red wine vinegar
1 tsp cornstarch
onion powder
hot sauce or cayenne pepper, to taste
agave nectar or raw sugar, to taste
ketchup, as needed

Chef's Note Each city has its own spin on patatas bravas. In many cities, patatas bravas are also served with mayo or some other aioli. Try mixing smoked paprika or chipotle powder (to taste) in Vegan Mayo (pg. 233) as an additional dipping sauce for the potatoes.

Preheat oven to 350°F. Line a baking sheet with parchment paper and place cubed potatoes on top. Bake until crispy and cooked thoroughly—about 20–25 minutes. For added crispness, I suggest switching to broil (high) at the end for a minute or two, but be careful—they can burn fast that way.

Meanwhile, make tomato sauce: Combine all ingredients (except ketchup and agave nectar) in a blender or food processor and blend until smooth and creamy. Transfer to a saucepan and bring to a boil, stirring constantly for about a minute. Turn off heat and remove pot from the hot stove—the sauce will thicken as it cools. When it does, taste, adding more hot sauce as desired. If it's a little too acidic or tart, add a little ketchup (about ½ tsp) or a tiny bit of agave nectar or raw sugar.

Pour tomato sauce over the potatoes when they're done baking and serve with toothpicks.

PER SERVING | Calories 98, Total Fat 0.1g, Carbohydrates 19.6g, Fiber 2.9g, Sugars 2.9g, Protein 2.1g

andrea's salt and vinegar potatoes

ENGLAND

My friend Andrea developed this recipe one afternoon to appease her cravings for malt vinegar potato chips. Scott went bonkers for these potatoes, and now I'm hooked too. They remind me of England's famous "fish and chips" since the "chips" in England are traditionally served with vinegar instead of ketchup.

Preheat oven to 350°F. Slice red potatoes into thin rounds and temporarily set aside. Create a pocket with aluminum foil and put the potatoes into it. (You are basically making a pouch for the potatoes.) Pour vinegar (about ½ c) into the pouch so that all of the potatoes are well coated. Bake for 35–40 minutes. When potatoes are almost done, fork-tender but not completely soft, remove from the oven. Drain off any excess vinegar and open aluminum foil pouch on a baking sheet. Spread the potatoes out so there is no overlap. Salt the potatoes generously and bake for another 10–20 minutes, or until they get a bit crunchier. Once they're done, douse them in a little more vinegar, plus additional salt, if desired.

SERVES 1

2 red potatoes
½ c apple cider vinegar
aluminum foil

Chef's Note White vinegar also works in this recipe.

PER SERVING | Calories 323, Total Fat 0.6g, Carbohydrates 68.9g, Fiber 7.2g, Sugars 4.7g, Protein 8.1g

NETHERLANDS

french fries

Fries, chips, *frites, patates frites, pommes frites* . . . it doesn't matter what you call them; fries are a popular street food in Europe. In Belgium (where fries originated) and the Netherlands, you can find fry stands called friteries and they always have a line around the corner, particularly at night! My favorite way to eat these oven-baked fries is with Curry Ketchup (pg. 191).

Preheat oven to 425°F. Line cookie sheet with parchment paper and set aside. Cut potato into fry-size strips about the size of your pinky finger. It's important they are as even in size as possible.

Bake 10 minutes, flipping after 7. Then switch to broil (high) for another minute or two, until golden—but careful, they can burn fast.

SERVES 1

1 potato

Chef's Note In the Netherlands (as well as the Dutch side of St. Maarten), fries are served with mayonnaise instead of ketchup.

Chef's Note I learned the "broil" trick from Jeff Novick, MS, RD, who makes potato wedges by broiling.

PER SERVING

Calories 131, Total Fat 0.1g, Carbohydrates 29.7g, Fiber 3.7g, Sugars 1.3g, Protein 3.4g

"cheater" african green beans

ETHIOPIA

UGANDA

I love African cuisine and here I'm blending key flavors from Ethiopia and Uganda with green beans. I call this recipe "cheater" since it uses a dab of peanut butter and is therefore not fat-free, but the hint of nutty flavor and creaminess really makes this dish.

Line a skillet with a thin layer of vegetable broth and sauté garlic and onion over high heat until garlic is golden and onion is soft and translucent, adding splashes of broth as needed. Meanwhile, in a measuring cup, whisk tomato sauce with ¼ c broth, Berberé, cumin, paprika, and Dijon mustard, and set aside. Once garlic and onions are done, add green beans, tomato sauce mixture, and remaining broth. Bring to a boil, then reduce heat to low, cover, and cook until beans are cooked and darker green but still crisp (the liquid should also have reduced). Meanwhile, mix flour with peanut butter and 2 tbsp water, whisking to combine, then add a minute before beans are done, stirring to coat. Add chickpea mixture about a minute before beans are done, stirring to coat. Allow sauce to thicken slightly, so it coats the beans but is not gloppy or runny. Taste, adding salt and pepper or more Berberé or cayenne.

SERVES 2

- 1 c vegetable broth, divided
- 6 garlic cloves, thinly sliced
- ½ small red onion, diced
- ¼ c tomato sauce
- ¼–½ tsp Berberé (pg. 231)
- ¼ tsp ground cumin
- ⅛ tsp paprika
- ½ tsp Dijon mustard
- ½ lb green beans, trimmed
- 1 tbsp chickpea flour
- ½ tsp smooth peanut butter

Chef's Note If using commercial berberé, start with less, as some brands are explosive with heat spices.

PER SERVING

Calories 103, Total Fat 1.5g, Carbohydrates 20.7g, Fiber 6.1g, Sugars 5g, Protein 4.9g

FRANCE

savory glazed carrots

▌▌ PRONUNCIATION TIP
Carottes vichy sounds like "care-rotts vish-she."

Carottes vichy is a classic French dish; it's basically butter-glazed carrots with a touch of sugar and herbs. I'm borrowing the herbed, semisweet glaze idea here; but instead of butter, I'm using my favorite French product: Dijon mustard. These carrots are so flavorful and a terrific (easy!) side dish that will complement any meal.

SERVES 2

- 1 tsp cornstarch
- vegetable broth, as needed
- 2 tsp Dijon mustard
- 1 tsp Italian seasoning
- ¼ tsp pure maple syrup
- 4 carrots, skinned and chopped

Mix cornstarch into 2 tbsp water and set aside. Line a skillet with a thin layer of broth. Whisk in mustard, Italian seasoning, and maple syrup. Add carrots and bring to a boil over high heat. Reduce to medium and sauté carrots until fork-tender or softer, about 4–5 minutes. Stir regularly and add more broth as needed to prevent sticking. Once carrots are cooked, check liquid, adding more broth as necessary. You want a thin lining of broth on the bottom. Reduce heat to low and stir in cornstarch slurry. Continue to cook, stirring constantly, until liquid thickens into a glaze and coats carrots. Serve warm.

PER SERVING | Calories 72, Total Fat 1.2g, Carbohydrates 15g, Fiber 3.6g, Sugars 6.8g, Protein 1.4g

spring rolls

THAILAND

Spring rolls are a popular appetizer in several Asian cuisines: Taiwanese, Chinese, Thai, Indonesian, and Vietnamese, just to name a few. The fillings often vary with the seasons, which is why you might see them referred to as both spring rolls and summer rolls. I've blended the flavors of Taiwanese, Vietnamese, and Thai spring rolls here to create the ultimate Asian-inspired appetizer.

Press tofu, then cut the block into 4 slabs. Cut each slab into 3 pieces (for a total of 12 sticks) and set aside. Use a dish or pan that's big enough to easily lay your spring roll wrapper in and fill with about ¼ inch water—enough water to cover 1 wrapper when completely submerged. Place 1 spring roll wrapper in cold water for 30–40 seconds (or according to package directions). If the wrapper is not soaked long enough, it is difficult to wrap; if it is soaked for too long, it can easily tear. Gently take the wrapper out of the water dish and let water drain off.

Place the wrapper on a flat surface, like a clean cutting board. Place 1 stick of tofu and a few pieces of carrot, cucumber, sprouts, and a little lettuce in the center. Pick up the bottom of wrapper and fold over the fillings. Then pick up one side and fold it over, repeating with the other side. Continue to roll wrapper all the way to the top. Set spring roll aside and repeat the process with remaining ingredients.

For a dipping sauce, use teriyaki sauce, sweet chili sauce, Thai Kitchen's Spicy Mango Sauce, or Satay Sauce (pg. 196).

SERVES 12

- ½ lb firm tofu
- 1½ c cooked brown rice
- 1 carrot, julienned
- ½ cucumber, julienned
- 1½ c lettuce, chopped
- 1 c sprouts
- 12 spring roll wrappers
  dipping sauce, to taste

Chef's Note I place the wrapper on a cutting board with the bottom hanging off the board. This makes it easier to pick up and roll the wrapper.

PER SERVING
(1 ROLL, WITHOUT DIPPING SAUCE)

Calories 143, Total Fat 1.6g, Carbohydrates 26.2g, Fiber 1.5g, Sugars 0.8g, Protein 6.2g

ITALY

lemony kale

Fresh lemon complements kale beautifully, and the sweet tang of balsamic vinegar adds a nice complexity to an otherwise simple dish. For a complete meal, add chickpeas.

SERVES 2

1 bunch kale

vegetable broth, as needed

5 garlic cloves, minced

½ small lemon (juice and zest)

balsamic vinegar, as needed

Remove stems from kale, tear leaves into bite-sized pieces, and set aside. Line skillet with a thin layer of broth and sauté garlic over high heat until it is golden, fragrant, and the broth has cooked off. Add enough additional broth so there is a very thin layer present and add kale. Continue to cook over high heat, stirring kale constantly until it softens and turns brighter in color, about 1–2 minutes. Also, make sure minced garlic is coating kale. Turn off heat and squeeze in lemon juice, stirring to combine. Then add balsamic vinegar and stir. Add a pinch of lemon zest and stir again, then serve.

PER SERVING | Calories 85, Total Fat 1.0g, Carbohydrates 18.2g, Fiber 2.9g, Sugars 0.7g, Protein 5.0g

edamame

FUN FACT The Japanese word *edamame* literally means "twig bean" (*eda* = twig, *mame* = bean).

I love edamame and it's easy enough to make at home, but for some reason my edamame never tasted quite like it did in a restaurant. I couldn't figure out what was different about restaurant edamame—until I saw it being cooked in Hawaii and noticed there was an onion floating in the water. Aha! That was it!

Bring a large pot of water to a boil. Once boiling, add onion half (unsliced) and simmer for about 5 minutes, until the onion starts to soften. Then add edamame and cook according to package instructions. Drain off water (discard onion) and sprinkle pods generously with sea salt. Squeeze fresh lemon juice over top and serve.

PER SERVING | Calories 77, Total Fat 2.2g, Carbohydrates 7.9g, Fiber 3.1g, Sugars 1.3g, Protein 5.8g

JAPAN

CHINA

HAWAII

SERVES 4

½ small onion
16 oz frozen edamame
sea salt (coarse)
lemon slices

Chef's Note As an alternative, I sometimes drizzle the pods with low-sodium soy sauce or teriyaki sauce instead of salt. Chinese 5-spice is also great sprinkled on edamame.

Amsterdam, The Netherlands (2007)

Amsterdam, The Netherlands (2011)

Amsterdam was not a city I ever intended to visit. Maybe it was pop culture or rumor, but I had developed an opinion that Amsterdam was filled with hookers and potheads, and while I generally try not to judge others or the activities that they engage in, those things just aren't for me.

However, fate had a different plan. I had to route through Amsterdam to get where I was going. I was annoyed and irritated but went nonetheless. Within minutes of arriving at Amsterdam Centraal railway station, I felt

Amsterdam, The Netherlands (2011)

Amsterdam, The Netherlands

like a jerk—and by the end of that day, I had egg on my face (no, not literally, though I certainly deserved it).

Amsterdam is exceptionally beautiful, with history and culture aplenty. I marveled at paintings I'd only seen as posters at the Van Gogh museum, walked through history, cried at the Anne Frank House, and came to appreciate the sexual revolution and its role in feminism at the Sex Museum. In short, there was so much more to Amsterdam than marijuana and prostitutes, and I realized I had been a fool for putting stock in stereotypes.

Amsterdam, The Netherlands (2011)

It was an unwitting reminder to me that you can't judge a book by its cover, that rumors are often untrue, and that I must base my opinions on my own experiences and not those of others.

Amsterdam remains one of my most favorite cities and one of only a few places I revisit during my trips abroad. During my last journey, I scribbled this message in my notebook: "In Amsterdam and remembering why this is perhaps my favorite city in the world. Even on a horribly wet, damp, and cool day, this place is beautiful, complicated, and perfect." (Dated 9/11/2011)

Amsterdam, The Netherlands (2011)

stir-fries & veggie dishes

THAILAND

bok choy delight

This Thai-inspired dish is flavorful, fast, and presents beautifully. For a full meal, toss in cubed tofu or shelled edamame and serve over cooked brown rice or quinoa.

SERVES 2

- 1 tbsp Dijon mustard
- 1 tbsp sweet red chili sauce
- red pepper flakes
- ½ tsp ground ginger
- 2 tbsp low-sodium soy sauce
- 1 tbsp rice vinegar
- 1 bunch green onions
- 6 garlic cloves, minced
- 1 large bok choy, chopped
- vegetable broth, as needed
- cornstarch slurry (1 tsp cornstarch mixed into 2 tbsp water)

Line a skillet with a thin layer of water. Whisk in Dijon, chili sauce, a pinch of red pepper flakes, ginger, soy sauce, and rice vinegar and set aside. Chop the rooty bottoms off the green onions and discard. Reserve dark green parts for later and mince white and light green parts. Add to skillet with garlic and sauté over high heat until most of the liquid has evaporated. Add bok choy and a splash of broth (there should always be a thin layer of liquid coating the skillet). Continue to cook, stirring constantly, until bok choy is fork-tender but still crisp. Add cornstarch slurry and allow to thicken. Toss to coat and garnish with sliced dark green onions.

PER SERVING | Calories 132, Total Fat 1.4g, Carbohydrates 24.5g, Fiber 6.1g, Sugars 10g, Protein 9g

Chef's Note You can use 2–3 baby bok choy in place of the large bok choy.

chili bok choy

THAILAND

While living in St. Maarten, I fell in love with bok choy and Asian-inspired stir-fries. This recipe is an extension of that passion, and this time I've borrowed flavors from Thai cuisine. It's a simple but flavorful dish. Serve over cooked brown rice or quinoa.

Slice bok choy lengthwise several times and set aside. Line a skillet with a thin layer of broth. Add soy sauce, sweet red chili sauce, and vinegar, stirring to combine. Add garlic and ginger and white and light green parts of green onions, if using. Sauté over high heat until fragrant and garlic has turned golden, about 2 minutes. Add bok choy, a splash more of broth if necessary (you want to keep a thin layer of liquid at all times), and continue to cook, stirring frequently to coat the bok choy, until it has softened and taken on a bit of a brown coloring, about 3 minutes. About a minute before bok choy is done, add cilantro, stirring to combine. Once bok choy is done, stir in leftover green onions, if using. You should still have a thin layer of liquid left; if not, add more broth. Toss around bok choy so it is coated well—the sauce is the best part! Add optional garnishes and serve.

SERVES 2

- 1 large bok choy
  vegetable broth
- 1 tbsp low-sodium soy sauce
- 2 tbsp sweet red chili sauce
- 1 tbsp rice vinegar
- 4 garlic cloves, minced
- 1–2 tsp fresh ginger, minced
- 2 tbsp cilantro, minced

OPTIONAL GARNISHES:

- 2–3 green onions, sliced
  sriracha
  raw cashews

Chef's Note You can use 2–3 baby bok choy in place of 1 large bok choy.

PER SERVING | Calories 113, Total Fat 1g, Carbohydrates 21.2g, Fiber 4.6g, Sugars 11.5g, Protein 7.3g

thai mango curry

THAILAND

One of my absolute favorite foods to eat in Maui was a creamy mango custard made from mango and coconut milk. I've captured that creamy sweet combination in this curry, while adding a little bit of heat and Thai flavors.

Remove rooty bottom from green onions, slice into 2-inch pieces, then slice those pieces in half longways. Add green onions to a skillet with ginger and garlic. Line skillet with a thin layer of water and sauté over high heat for a minute or so, until garlic and ginger are fragrant and green onions have softened. Add bell peppers, plus more water if necessary to line the bottom of the pan, and continue to cook over high heat until bell peppers are tender, but still crisp. Turn off heat and set aside. Take about ¼–⅓ of the cubed mango and pulverize it in a blender or food processor, adding a splash of water if necessary. Add the blended mango, remaining mango cubes, coconut milk, soy sauce, and sweet chili sauce to the skillet, stirring to combine. Heat over low until thoroughly warm and serve over rice. Add sriracha, if desired, and garnish with cilantro.

SERVES 2

- 6 green onions
- 1 tbsp fresh ginger, minced
- 3 garlic cloves, minced
- 1 red bell pepper, seeded and sliced
- 1 yellow bell pepper, seeded and sliced
- 1 mango, skin removed and cubed
- ½ c lite coconut milk
- ½ tsp low-sodium soy sauce
- 2 tbsp sweet red chili sauce
- 2 tbsp cilantro, minced
- cooked brown rice
- sriracha (optional)
- green onion (optional)

Chef's Note For a lower fat version, replace half of the coconut milk with sweetened nondairy milk or use all nondairy milk with a drop of coconut extract.

PER SERVING (WITHOUT RICE) | Calories 199, Total Fat 3.9g, Carbohydrates 39.9g, Fiber 6.0g, Sugars 27.5g, Protein 3.9g

THAILAND

thai pineapple curry

This curry has just the right sweet-to-heat ratio and is bursting with Thai flavors. For a complete meal, add cubed tofu and serve over cooked brown rice.

SERVES 2

- 4 green onions, sliced
- 1 tbsp ginger, minced
- 2–3 garlic cloves, minced
- ¼ c vegetable broth
- 1 red bell pepper, seeded and sliced into thin strips
- ½–1 red finger pepper, seeded and sliced
- red pepper flakes, to taste
- 1 8-oz can diced pineapple (in juice, not syrup)
- 1¼ tsp mild yellow curry powder
- ½ c lite coconut milk
- 2 tbsp fresh basil, minced
- ½ tsp low-sodium soy sauce
- green onions (garnish)

Chef's Note For a lower-fat option, see note on pg. 93 (Thai Mango Curry).

Set aside a few dark green onion slices for garnish. Transfer the rest of the onions to a skillet with ginger and garlic. Add enough broth so there is a thin lining on the bottom of the skillet and sauté over high heat for a minute or two, until onion, ginger, and garlic are fragrant. Add red bell pepper and red finger pepper (or red pepper flakes as desired) and sauté until bell peppers start to soften, adding splashes of broth as necessary to prevent sticking. Once bell peppers start to soften, add pineapple with juices, stirring to combine. Cook another minute, until peppers are cooked but still somewhat crisp and pineapple is warm. Meanwhile, in a measuring cup or small bowl, whisk curry powder into coconut milk, then pour into skillet and stir to combine. After 30 seconds, add basil and soy sauce, stirring again to combine. Taste, adding more soy sauce or basil if desired. Garnish with green onions, lime wedges, and a basil leaf or two.

PER SERVING | Calories 155, Total Fat 3.6g, Carbohydrates 30.7g, Fiber 3.7g, Sugars 20.3g, Protein 2.7g

MEXICO

stuffed poblanos

SERVES 2

2 poblano peppers
vegetable broth
1 green bell pepper, seeded and diced
1 small onion, diced
1 tsp chili powder
½ tsp ground cumin
¼ tsp dried oregano or marjoram
cayenne pepper (optional)
½ c kidney, black, or pinto beans
½ c salsa

PER POBLANO

Calories 132, Total Fat 1.3g, Carbohydrates 25.8g, Fiber 7.2g, Sugars 8.5g, Protein 6.7g

Friends of mine went to Mexico and came back raving about the incredible stuffed poblanos they had on vacation. I loved the idea of stuffed poblanos, so I created this Mexican-inspired dish that uses key Mexican ingredients and flavors stuffed into a baked poblano. If you don't have access to poblano peppers, a bell pepper is a fine substitute.

Preheat oven to 350°F. Place poblanos on a cookie sheet and bake 10–20 minutes, or until they have softened. Meanwhile, line a skillet with a thin layer of vegetable broth and sauté bell pepper and onion over high heat for a minute or so. Add chili powder, cumin, oregano, and cayenne, if desired, and continue to sauté until onions are translucent, bell pepper is soft and a deeper green, and spices are fragrant, about 3 minutes more. Add splashes of broth as necessary to prevent sticking. Turn off heat and stir in salsa and beans until well combined. When poblanos are done, slice lengthwise down the middle of one side and use a spoon to scoop out the seeds. *Immediately wash your hands!* Spoon bean–bell pepper mixture into poblanos and return to oven. Bake 2–5 more minutes, just to warm them up.

Chef's Note If your poblanos refuse to soften, try broiling them for a few minutes.

pesto-stuffed mushrooms

ITALY

Pesto sauce comes from northern Italy and is traditionally made with pine nuts, garlic, basil, oil, and Parmesan cheese. Here, I've lightened up classic pesto by using white beans instead of pine nuts. Although this version still tastes like pesto, the resulting sauce is a little too thick for pasta, but its thickness makes it perfect for spreading on crusty Italian bread or stuffing into mushrooms. For a more authentic pesto pasta sauce, see Quick Pesto (pg. 182).

Preheat oven to 350°F. Combine beans, basil, garlic, and wine in a food processor or blender and pulse until smooth and well combined. Taste, adding more basil if desired, plus salt and pepper to taste. Stuff pesto into mushrooms and place mushrooms in a muffin tin or on a silicone mat and bake 10–15 minutes, until mushrooms are tender but not mushy or falling apart. Garnish each mushroom with a sliced black olive or a dash of vegan Parmesan, if desired. Serve warm, not piping hot.

12 MUSHROOMS

- ⅔ c cooked or canned white beans
- 1 c fresh basil, packed
- 1 garlic clove
- 3 tbsp white wine
- 12 white mushrooms, stems removed
- black olives, sliced (optional)
- vegan Parmesan cheese (optional)

Chef's Note These mushrooms can be prepared in advance. Stuff, store in fridge, and heat later.

Chef's Note Any white beans will do here, such as cannellini, navy, or butter beans.

PER MUSHROOM Calories 19, Total Fat 0.2g, Carbohydrates 2.7g, Fiber 0.8g, Sugars 0g, Protein 1.3g

INDIA

vegetable korma

There are two ways to make this delicious Mughlai dish. One is creamy, like a curry, and the other is more reminiscent of traditional dry Indian dishes such as *Aloo Matar* (pg. 102) or *Aloo Gobi* (pg. 109). Serve the curry version over cooked brown rice and the dry version on its own.

SERVES 2

vegetable broth

¼ onion, sliced

5 garlic cloves, minced

1 potato, skinned and diced

2–3 carrots, skinned and sliced

1 tsp ground coriander

½ tsp ground cumin

cayenne pepper, to taste

¼ tsp turmeric

½ c tomato sauce

½ c frozen peas

¼ tsp garam masala

FOR THE CURRY VERSION

½ c nondairy milk

⅛ tsp coriander

⅛ tsp ground cumin

cayenne pepper, to taste

Line a medium pot with a thin layer of vegetable broth and sauté onions and garlic over high heat. Add more broth to reline the pot, plus potato and carrots. Sauté for another 3 minutes, then add coriander, cumin, cayenne as desired, and a couple dashes of turmeric, stirring to combine. Add tomato sauce, bring to a boil, and reduce to low. Cover and simmer until vegetables are fork-tender, about 5–10 more minutes, keeping a thin layer of liquid at all times. Add peas, stir to combine, and heat for another minute or two to warm up the peas. Add ⅛ tsp garam masala and stir to combine. Taste, adding more garam masala or more cayenne.

For a creamy curry, stir in ½ c nondairy milk, plus ⅛ tsp coriander and ⅛ tsp cumin, and more salt or cayenne (or garam masala—I often add another ¼ tsp) if desired.

CURRY VERSION Calories 180, Total Fat 1.4g, Carbohydrates 36.1g, Fiber 7.5g, Sugars 8.2g, Protein 6.8g

PER SERVING Calories 170, Total Fat 0.7g, Carbohydrates 35.6g, Fiber 7.3g, Sugars 8.2g, Protein 6.6 g

INDIA

aloo matar

Aloo matar is a popular Punjabi dish made of potatoes (*aloo*) and peas (*matar*) in flavorful tomato sauce. Serve with roti, naan, or cooked brown rice.

SERVES 2

- ½ c vegetable broth, divided
- 1 small onion, diced
- 1 tbsp fresh ginger, minced
- 1 tbsp garlic, minced
- ½ c tomato sauce
- 2 potatoes, cubed
- ¼ tsp mild curry powder
- ½ tsp paprika
- ½–1 tsp garam masala
- 1 c frozen peas
- 2 tbsp ketchup
- fresh cilantro, chopped (garnish)

Line a medium pot with a thin layer of broth and sauté onion, ginger, and garlic over high heat until onions are translucent, about 1 minute. Add tomato sauce, potatoes, and remaining broth, plus curry and paprika, stirring to combine. Bring to a boil, cover, and reduce to low. Simmer until potatoes are fork-tender, stirring periodically, about 10 minutes. Add ½ tsp garam masala plus peas and continue to cook until peas are warm. Add ketchup and stir to combine. Garnish with fresh cilantro, if desired.

PER SERVING | Calories 280, Total Fat 1.3g, Carbohydrates 59.2g, Fiber 11.8g, Sugars 14g, Protein 11g

vegetable enchiladas

These enchiladas are easy and quick to make and the best part is the enchilada sauce!

Preheat oven to 350°F. Line a 13x9 glass baking dish with a thin layer of Enchilada Sauce and set aside. Sauté onions with cumin in a little Enchilada Sauce over high heat for a minute or two, then add bell peppers and continue to cook until peppers soften. Once warm, set aside.

Pour ½ c Enchilada Sauce into a shallow dish, such as a pie dish, and dip tortillas so both sides are covered with sauce. Add vegetables, roll up and place crease-side-down in the baking dish. Repeat. Once enchiladas are assembled, pour remaining sauce over top. Bake 10–30 minutes (longer for crispier enchiladas) and serve with Quick Queso.

MEXICO

SERVES 6

Enchilada Sauce (pg. 201)

1 small onion, diced

1 tsp ground cumin

1 red bell pepper, seeded and sliced thin

1 green bell pepper, seeded and sliced thin

1 c frozen corn

1 c black beans

6 tortillas

Quick Queso (pg. 198) (optional)

PER SERVING
(WITHOUT QUICK QUESO)

Calories 287, Total Fat 2.6g, Carbohydrates 56.3g, Fiber 11.1g, Sugars 5.3g, Protein 13.4g

moroccan vegetables

MOROCCO

Tagine (also spelled *tajine*) is one of Morocco's most popular vegetarian dishes, though if you travel to Morocco, don't always assume vegetable *tagine* is vegetarian; it may be cooked in a lamb-based broth. Nevertheless, *tagine* is aromatic and delicious, and 20-some different ingredients could show up in any given recipe! (I have to applaud recipes where anything goes!) In my interpretation of *tagine*, I kept it simple with basic vegetables and core Moroccan spices. Serve *tagine* over quinoa or whole wheat couscous. For a complete meal, add chickpeas.

In a measuring cup, whisk broth with tomato paste, a few dashes of cinnamon and ginger, cumin, coriander, and paprika until well combined. Line a skillet with a thin layer of the broth mixture and sauté onions and carrots over high heat until onions are softer and translucent. Add remaining broth and vegetables, plus raisins, stirring to combine. Once boiling, cover and reduce to low and simmer until vegetables are fork-tender but not mush, about 5–7 minutes. Enough liquid should be left to coat everything, but if not, add a splash of water or vegetable broth. Add cayenne as desired plus salt to taste.

SERVES 2

- 1 c vegetable broth
- 1 tbsp tomato paste
- ground cinnamon
- ground ginger
- ½ tsp ground cumin
- ½ tsp ground coriander
- ¼ tsp paprika
- ½ red onion, diced
- 1 carrot, skinned and sliced
- 1 zucchini, sliced
- 1 yellow squash, sliced
- ¼ c raisins, chopped
- cayenne pepper

PER SERVING | Calories 127, Total Fat 0.7g, Carbohydrates 30.5g, Fiber 4.7g, Sugars 18.3g, Protein 4.0g

AFRICA

african delight

This warm and comforting one-pot meal is a fusion of Ethiopian and West African cuisine.

SERVES 2

- 1 bunch kale
- ½ c vegetable broth
- ½ red onion, sliced
- 1 sweet potato, cubed
- 2 tsp Berberé (pg. 231), divided
- 1 15-oz can white beans (any kind), drained and rinsed
- smoked paprika

Chef's Note If using commercial berberé, you might want to start with ½ tsp; some brands are explosive.

Chef's Note Any white bean can be used here, but I prefer navy or cannelini.

Tear leaves from kale stems, discarding stems. Tear kale leaves into bite-size pieces and set aside. Line a large pot with broth and add onion, sweet potato, and 1 tsp Berberé. Bring to a boil, cover, and reduce to low. Simmer until onions are translucent and potatoes are fork-tender, about 5–7 minutes. (The time varies based on how big or small you diced—check periodically and add more broth as necessary.) Once potatoes are fork-tender, stir in kale until it softens and turns darker in color, about 1–2 minutes. Then stir in beans and remaining 1 tsp Berberé. Taste, adding more Berberé if desired, plus salt to taste (optional). Sprinkle a few dashes of smoked paprika over top before serving.

PER SERVING | Calories 281, Total Fat 1.1g, Carbohydrates 61.3g, Fiber 17.9g, Sugars 5.1g, Protein 16.8g

aloo gobi

Aloo gobi is a popular Indian dish made of potatoes (*aloo*) and cauliflower (*gobi*).

INDIA

Line a medium pot with a thin layer of vegetable broth and sauté ginger, garlic, and onion over high heat until onions are translucent. Add tomato sauce, then stir in coriander, cumin, a few dashes of turmeric for color, plus a dash or two paprika and ketchup. Then add potato and cauliflower, and stir to coat everything well. Add remaining broth and stir again. Cover and bring to a boil. Once boiling, reduce to low and simmer 20 minutes—or until vegetables are fork-tender and soft. Add 1 tsp garam masala and cayenne as desired. Taste, adding salt or more garam masala as needed. Serve over cooked brown rice if desired and garnish generously with chopped cilantro.

SERVES 2

- 1 c vegetable broth, divided
- 1 tbsp fresh ginger, minced
- 2–3 garlic cloves, minced
- 1 small onion, diced
- 8 oz tomato sauce
- 1 tsp ground coriander
- ½ tsp ground cumin
- turmeric
- paprika
- 1 tbsp ketchup
- 1 brown potato, diced
- 1 head cauliflower, chopped into florets
- 1 tsp garam masala
- cayenne pepper, to taste
- cilantro, chopped (garnish)

PER SERVING   Calories 172, Total Fat 0.8g, Carbohydrates 38.5g, Fiber 8.1g, Sugars 12.5g, Protein 6.9g

insalata fantasia

ITALY

There are two things—well, three things—that I love about Italian grocery stores: 1) Their artisan bread selection is always outstanding with plenty of whole-grain options; 2) They carry soy yogurt, and, even better, soy ice cream; and 3) they have premade salads "to go" that are vegan. My favorite of the bunch is the Insalata Fantasia, and it is certainly a fantasy!

SERVES 1

3 c chopped lettuce
2–3 radishes, thinly sliced
5 black olives
5 green olives
1 c cherry tomatoes
⅓ c corn
lemon (optional)

Place lettuce in a serving bowl, then top with other vegetables (except lemon). Squeeze lemon over top.

Chef's Note I loved this salad served plain with fresh lemon juice squeezed over top. A light Italian dressing or my Balsamic Vinaigrette dressing (below) also works well with this salad.

balsamic vinaigrette

Whisk 2 tsp Dijon mustard with 1 tsp balsamic vinegar, 1 tsp red wine vinegar, and 1 tbsp water. Add a few drops or more of agave nectar to cut the tartness, to taste.

PER SERVING (WITHOUT DRESSING) Calories 246, Total Fat 13.5g, Carbohydrates 32.2g, Fiber 10.7g, Sugars 9.0g, Protein 4.7g

Brussels, Belgium (2011)

Salzburg, Austria (2011)

I love randomness in my travels. Right after I landed in Paris, I caught a train to Brussels. Once there, I came aboveground from the subway and found I had landed smack in the middle of a street parade. From there, I headed to the city center, where I was greeted by an orchestra playing my absolute favorite musical piece (the overture from *E.T.*) in the square. No amount of planning can compare to a serendipitous moment like that. I felt as though Europe and the universe were saying "Welcome home!"

Venice, Italy (2011)

Salzburg, Austria (2011)

A week later I convinced my husband and best friend that we should pit stop for a few hours in Salzburg, Austria, on our way to Croatia. We stepped off the train and directly into a citywide carnival. Salzburg was totally alive and beating with a singular pulse.

Still more surprises—a few days later we arrived in Milan, Italy, during Fashion Week (totally unplanned). Scott and I walked around the city for hours. At one point we wandered into a park where I spotted a curious outdoor bar. The "tables" looked like triangular UFOs (see inset on next page), and I just had to sit in one.

Milan, Italy (2011)

Venice, Italy (2011). Eating vegan gelato on my 30th birthday!

To get there, we had to go through a museum that had the most astonishing art and fashion exhibit—all of which was free. The exhibits were high-tech and interactive; one of the exhibits involved walking into a giant purse to get the experience of what it might feel like to be your keys. Another exhibit had a green backdrop so you could actually pose like a model and still another involved intertwined mosaics.

Moments like these are what make flying by the seat of your pants so fantastic.

grain-based dishes

CYPRUS

mama d's spanakorizo

PRONUNCIATION TIP
Spanakorizo sounds like "spah-nah-kore-ee-zoe."

SERVES 3

- 2¼ c vegetable broth, divided
- 1 large onion, diced
- 4–5 green onions, sliced
- 1 10-oz bag fresh spinach
- 1 15-oz can tomato sauce
- ¾ c uncooked brown rice
- 2 tsp dried dill
- lemon juice, to taste

This recipe is courtesy of my good friend Andrea's mom (we call her Mama Diddy) who is from Cyprus. Andrea says: "In Greek, *spanaki* is spinach and *rizi* is rice. . . . Who said Greek is complicated?"

Line a large pot with a thin layer of broth (about ¼ c) and sauté both types of onion over high heat until translucent and most of the liquid has cooked off. Add spinach and a splash of broth if necessary, and continue to cook, stirring the spinach until it cooks down and is slightly wilted. Turn off the heat and add tomato sauce, stirring to combine. Then add brown rice, remaining 2 c broth, and dill. Stir so the ingredients are just barely combined, but be careful not to overstir. (Less is more here; it will look soupy.) Cover and cook over low heat for 30–45 minutes, checking periodically to make sure the liquid doesn't run out, causing the rice to burn. Once the brown rice is cooked and fluffy, turn off the heat but leave the pot resting for another 15 minutes. Add salt and pepper to taste and a tiny squeeze of fresh lemon juice on top before serving.

PER SERVING | Calories 274, Total Fat 2.1g, Carbohydrates 58.9g, Fiber 8g, Sugars 10.4g, Protein 9.5g

polenta

ITALY

Although polenta is widely regarded as an Italian food (it has Italian peasant origins and rose to popularity during Roman times), it exists in several other international cuisines, sometimes with a different name or spelling. For example, in Serbia and parts of Croatia, it is called *palenta*.

Serve polenta as a side dish, or use it as a foundation for a meal by serving cooked vegetables and legumes on top of the soft and creamy polenta.

Bring 2 c water to a boil. Once boiling, reduce to low and slowly whisk in cornmeal. The mixture will start to clump; keep stirring or whisking so that it's smooth and homogeneous. Add splashes of nondairy milk or water as necessary to thin out the polenta and make it as creamy as you want. I usually add about ½ c nondairy milk. You can also drizzle in a little maple syrup (about 1 tbsp) for a sweeter polenta.

Spoon polenta into four bowls and garnish with a dash or two of smoked paprika. Then spoon desired topping over it and garnish with green onions.

SERVES 4

- 1 c cornmeal
- ½ c nondairy milk, as needed
- 1 tbsp pure maple syrup (optional)
- smoked paprika (garnish)
- green onions (garnish)

Chef's Note You can use either yellow or white cornmeal in this recipe. I find cornmeal with a sand-grain texture is best (not to be confused with coarse cornmeal), but the floury kind of cornmeal also works.

PER SERVING

JUST CORNMEAL Calories 110, Total Fat 1.1g, Carbohydrates 23.4g, Fiber 2.2g, Sugar 0g, Protein 2.5g

WITH ½ C NONDAIRY MILK AND 1 TBSP MAPLE SYRUP Calories 128, Total Fat 1.5g, Carbohydrates 27.1g, Fiber 2.4g, Sugar 3.2g, Protein 2.6g

tostada con tomate

SPAIN

PRONUNCIATION TIP
Tostada con tomate sounds like "toe-stah-da con toe-maht-tay."

Tostada con tomate (toast with tomato) is the most popular breakfast in Spain. If you walk by a café in the morning, you'll see Spaniards eating it with a *Café con Leche* (pg. 216). Because it's vegan, I had *tostada con tomate* many mornings in Spain. Traditionally, olive oil is drizzled on top, but I find a little bit of juice from the olive bottle captures the flavor just fine.

Rub tomatoes against a cheese grater, discarding skins. Add a pinch of salt, plus a dash or two of garlic powder (or as much as you like), plus a little drizzle of liquid from a jar of green olives or capers. Stir to combine and slather on toasted bread.

SERVES 1

1–2 plum tomatoes

garlic powder (granulated)

green olive or caper brine

toast

Chef's Note Some Spaniards rub fresh garlic on their tostada before spreading the tomato mixture or use oil infused with garlic. I can't wake up and eat raw garlic, but I do like the taste of garlic and tomatoes, which is why I use garlic powder.

PER SERVING
(WITHOUT BREAD, 2 TOMATOES) | Calories 58, Total Fat 0.5g, Carbohydrates 12.8g, Fiber 2.7g, Sugars 9.9g, Protein 3g

ITALY

roasted tomato pilaf

Rice-based dishes, typically called pilafs, exist in several cuisines: Middle Eastern, Caribbean, East African, and Latin American, just to name a few. Here I have created a pilaf using southern Italian and Mediterranean flavors. For a full meal, add chickpeas.

SERVES 2

- 10 oz cherry tomatoes
- ¼ c vegetable broth
- 3 garlic cloves, minced
- 2–3 c spinach, chopped
- 1 c cooked brown rice, warmed
- balsamic vinegar (optional)

Preheat oven to 350°F. Line a cookie sheet with parchment paper and place tomatoes on the cookie sheet, spread out. Bake 5–10 minutes, until tomatoes are wrinkled. Once tomatoes are done, line a skillet with a thin layer of vegetable broth and sauté garlic over high heat until it turns golden and fragrant, about 2–3 minutes. (Some, but not all, of the broth will evaporate.) Add spinach and stir a few times so the spinach cooks lightly but is still brilliant in color. Stir in cooked rice, then gently fold in tomatoes. Season with salt and pepper to taste. Drizzle balsamic vinegar over top, if desired.

PER SERVING | Calories 149, Total Fat 1.3g, Carbohydrates 31.0g, Fiber 4.2g, Sugars 4.4g, Protein 4.9g

MEXICO

easy spanish rice

SERVES 4

- 1 c uncooked brown rice
- 2 c vegetable broth or water
- ¼–⅓ c salsa or marinara sauce

Chef's Note Although this dish is known as Spanish rice in the United States, it doesn't exist in Spain and is actually from Mexico, where it's called simply *arroz* (rice).

Without fail, I always have a bit of salsa or pasta sauce left over, lingering in my fridge. I can't seem to bring myself to throw it out, but I also wonder, "What the heck am I going to make with so little sauce?" Well, I've found my answer. This rice reminds me of Spanish rice, only it's a much easier version. To extend this dish, stir in mixed cooked vegetables like peas, carrots, or corn. Chopped cilantro or parsley and green onion also make a great garnish.

Combine all ingredients together. Cover and bring to a boil. Reduce to low and simmer 40 minutes, or until rice is cooked and liquid has absorbed. Add salt and pepper to taste, if desired.

PER SERVING
(ABOUT 1/3 CUP)

Calories 196, Total Fat 2g, Carbohydrates 37.7g, Fiber 1.9g, Sugars 0.8g, Protein 6.2g

paella

PRONUNCIATION TIP
Paella sounds like "pie-yay-yauh."

SPAIN

Paella is a Valencian rice dish that can be found throughout Spain. Although most paellas involve some kind of seafood, you can find vegetarian paella fairly easily as well.

Whiz 1 c tomatoes, 2 c broth, and tomato paste until smooth in a blender and set aside. Line a large, flat skillet with a thin layer of broth and sauté garlic, onions, and bell pepper over high heat until most of the water has cooked off and garlic is golden. Add remaining tomatoes and stir to combine. Turn off heat, add rice, and stir-fry for 2 minutes. Pour tomato mixture in and stir to combine. Cover, bring to a boil and simmer until the liquid has absorbed, about 40 minutes to 1 hour—but check it so it doesn't burn. (Paella rice is usually served al dente.) If your rice isn't finished after the first hour or you prefer it more cooked, slowly drizzle ½ to 1 c water in a clockwise fashion (don't disturb the rice). Cover, bring to a boil, then simmer until liquid has absorbed. Garnish with paprika and drizzle with fresh lemon juice before eating.

SERVES 2

- 1 15-oz can fire-roasted tomatoes, divided
- 2¼ c vegetable broth, divided
- 1 tbsp tomato paste
- 5 garlic cloves, minced
- 3 green onions
- 1 red bell pepper, seeded and diced
- ¾ c brown rice
  smoked paprika (garnish)
  lemon wedges (juice)

Chef's Note The secret to paella is not to disturb the rice.

PER SERVING | Calories 366, Total Fat 2.2g, Carbohydrates 77.5g, Fiber 6.3g, Sugars 11.8g, Protein 8.6g

african jollof

AFRICA

Jollof rice, also called *benachin*, is a popular dish throughout West Africa, particularly in Ghana and Nigeria. Many variations to this dish exist, but core ingredients include rice, tomato paste, onion, and a medley of vegetables and spices.

Pour tomato sauce into a pot, then add enough broth so liquid completely covers the bottom. Add onions, a dash or two cinnamon, cumin, chili powder, and curry powder, then sauté over high heat until onions are translucent, about 1 minute. Turn heat down to low and add frozen vegetables, stirring to warm them. Continue to cook over low heat and stir frequently until vegetables are warm. Add cooked rice and stir to completely combine. As you are stirring, the rice should take on a dark coloring. Add 1 more tbsp tomato sauce, plus salt and black pepper to taste. For a spicier dish, add hot sauce to taste.

SERVES 4

- ¼ c plus 1 tbsp tomato sauce, divided
- vegetable broth, as needed
- 1 small onion, diced small
- ground cinnamon
- ½ tsp ground cumin
- ½ tsp chili powder
- ¼ tsp mild curry powder
- 2 c frozen mixed vegetables
- 1½ c cooked brown rice
- hot sauce (optional)

PER SERVING | Calories 161, Total Fat 1.0g, Carbohydrates 33.4g, Fiber 6.3g, Sugars 5.3g, Protein 5.2g

THAILAND

orange teriyaki rice

I was first introduced to orange teriyaki when I was staying with my friend's family in Maui one summer. Hawaii has a large Asian population; so many dishes are a fusion of Asian and Hawaiian cuisine. Although orange teriyaki sauce is more commonly used as a marinade for chicken or pork in Hawaii, I kept thinking it would be delicious paired with brown rice. It absolutely is! This rice side is so easy to prepare and packs a lot of flavor! To fill out the meal, add cubed tofu or shelled edamame.

SERVES 1 OR 2

- 1 c cooked brown rice
- 1 tbsp teriyaki sauce
- ½ orange (juice and zest)
- 1 green onion, sliced

Combine rice with teriyaki sauce, stirring to coat rice with sauce. Taste, adding more teriyaki sauce if desired. Add 1 tsp orange zest and juice from two slices of the orange. Stir to combine. Taste, adding more juice or zest for a more citrus flavor if desired. Stir in green onion and serve.

PER SERVING

SERVES 1 Calories 282, Total Fat 1.8g, Carbohydrates 60.6g, Fiber 6.1g, Sugars 11.5g, Protein 6.7g

SERVES 2 Calories 141, Total Fat 0.9g, Carbohydrates 30.3g, Fiber 3.1g, Sugars 5.7g, Protein 3.4g

tabbouleh

LEBANON

Tabbouleh needs no introduction. Like hummus, tabbouleh is a popular ethnic food in the United States, and it makes a great snack, appetizer, or light lunch. Although tabbouleh is traditionally made with bulgur wheat, I'm using quinoa here for a gluten-free option. Plus, I always have quinoa on hand, but I almost never stock bulgur wheat in my pantry.

Mix together all ingredients, stirring to combine. Taste, adding more lemon or brine if desired. You can also add salt or black or white pepper if desired. Cover with plastic wrap and chill for at least 1 hour.

SERVES 5
(MAKES 2½ CUPS)

- 2 c cooked quinoa
- ⅔ c fresh parsley, minced
- ¼ c fresh mint, minced
- 3–4 garlic cloves, minced
- 3–5 green onions, minced
- ½ small lemon (juice)
- 1–2 tbsp brine from green olives

PER SERVING
(ABOUT ½ CUP)

Calories 72, Total Fat 1.1g, Carbohydrates 13.2g, Fiber 2.0g, Sugars 0.5g, Protein 3.0g

Chef's Note You can also add tomatoes and cucumbers to tabbouleh, but wait to add them just before serving.

SWITZERLAND

müesli

I stayed with a Herbie in Hamburg, and every morning she made me this wonderful müesli for breakfast. It consisted of plain soy yogurt, rolled oats, flax seeds, and chopped fresh fruit (peaches, grapes, and bananas). I really loved it. I then came across müesli again in Switzerland, where it originates. Swiss physician Maximilian Bircher-Benner invented müesli, though how we eat it today isn't very reflective of his recipe. The original recipe involved soaking oats in water, then mixing them with a little cream, lemon juice, and grated apple. This recipe still involves soaking oats and it's creamy, but it's more like the dish I enjoyed in Germany.

SERVES 1

⅓ c rolled oats
½–⅔ c nondairy milk
fresh fruit, diced

Chef's Note While oats themselves are gluten-free, many brands are cross-contaminated. For a truly gluten-free option, use certified gluten-free oats.

PER SERVING
(WITH ½ CUP NONDAIRY MILK [WITHOUT FRUIT])

Calories 123, Total Fat 3.3g, Carbohydrates 19.5g, Fiber 3.2g, Sugars 0g, Protein 4.1g

Combine oats with nondairy milk (⅔ c makes it a little soupy, which I prefer). Chill overnight, or for at least 2 hours. It gets thick, almost like yogurt. Stir in diced fresh fruit such as apple, pear, peach, banana, grapes, or strawberries before serving and enjoy.

Hamburg, Germany (2011)

JAPAN

sushi rice

In Japan, the term "sushi" refers to a vinegar-seasoned rice, not the rolls we think of in the United States. Use this rice as a side dish to any Asian-inspired meal or add other ingredients like sliced green onion, diced yellow bell pepper, sprouts, cubed tofu, cucumber, avocado, etc., to make a "sushi rice bowl" meal.

SERVES 2

- ½ c uncooked brown rice
- ⅓ c rice vinegar
- 2 tbsp raw sugar
- 1 tsp sea salt
- kelp (optional)

Put rice in a pot with 1 c water. Cover, bring to a boil, then simmer on low until rice is cooked and water has evaporated, about 40 minutes. Meanwhile, combine vinegar, sugar, salt, and a few dashes of kelp, if desired, together in a saucepan and bring to a near boil, removing before it boils and when sugar and salt dissolve. This mixture is called *sushi-zu*. Mix cooked rice with *sushi-zu*. If you don't use all of it, *sushi-zu* stores indefinitely in an airtight container.

PER SERVING | Calories 247, Total Fat 1.3g, Carbohydrates 48.8g, Fiber 1.6g, Sugars 12.6g, Protein 3.6g

hand rolls

Hand rolls are called *temaki* (手巻) in Japanese. They have the same ingredients as sushi but are prepared differently. You have a cone made of nori with both the rice and fillings inside. Hand rolls are much easier to prepare than cut sushi rolls and the flavor possibilities are endless!

JAPAN

Cut each nori sheet into quarters and set aside. Prepare fillings. Fill a small bowl with water and have it handy. Carefully fold one piece of nori into a cone shape. Wet your finger and run it along overlapping parts; the wetness will make it stick together and form a cone. Stuff the cone with rice and your chosen fillings.

Some of my favorite combos are tofu and teriyaki sauce; tofu and sweet red chili sauce; red or yellow bell pepper, avocado, mango, and avocado; cucumber and ginger; cucumber and carrot; cucumber and sprouts; green apple and agave (it's not gross, I swear!); or just plain rice with a flavorful sauce, such as teriyaki or sweet red chili sauce. I usually add the rice and filling, then put a little dab of "sauce" on top.

MAKES 8

2 nori sheets

1 c cooked brown rice or Sushi Rice (pg. 136)

fillings of your choice

Chef's Note *Temaki* must be eaten immediately for the best taste and texture. The nori cone absorbs moisture from the filling as it sits, causing the cone to lose its crispness and become chewy and difficult to bite.

PER HAND ROLL [WITHOUT FILLING] | Calories 46, Total Fat 0.3g, Carbohydrates 9.1g, Fiber 0.7g, Sugar 0g, Protein 1.2g

THAILAND

pineapple rice

Pineapple rice is one of my favorite Thai dishes, though it's often fried and prepared with fish sauce. Enter this much healthier and vegan version. It's a great side to any Asian-inspired meal, or you can turn it into a full meal by adding cubed tofu or edamame.

SERVES 1

1 c cooked brown rice

2 tbsp pineapple juice (from the can)

¼ c crushed pineapple

2 green onions, sliced

1 tbsp fresh basil, minced

½ tsp low-sodium soy sauce

Mix warm rice with all ingredients until well mixed. Taste, adding more soy sauce if desired.

PER SERVING | Calories 266, Total Fat 1.8g, Carbohydrates 57.4g, Fiber 4.9g, Sugars 7.7g, Protein 5.6g

Chef's Note For a twist, use teriyaki sauce instead of soy sauce.

Granada (Alhambra), Spain (2011)

Granada (Alhambra), Spain (2011)

I was hopelessly lost in Granada. The address for my hostel was confusing, and I had forgotten to write down the telephone number when I made online reservations the night before. I had asked dozens of strangers for help, but no one knew where my hostel was or even had a clue where on my map was the address I needed. Feeling defeated (and lost!), I wandered around Granada for an hour hoping to find an Internet café so I could look up the hostel and my reservation. Unfortunately for me, it was siesta and everything was closed.

Granada (Alhambra), (2011)

I rested against the wall just outside of a closed Internet café and scanned my map, hoping to find the elusive hostel.

That's when Pablo spotted me. He came over asking if I needed help. Pablo looked at the map and the address and was equally confused. Then he asked if I wanted to use his Internet. Turns out I was sitting on his doorstep!

Pablo (and his Internet!) helped me find my way, and he also invited me out later that night to meet up with him and his friends at a local bar that—get ready for this—happened to have an entire vegan menu! (Yes, I nearly died.)

Granada, Spain (2011)

Granada, Spain (2011)

Granada, Spain (2011)

It was a fantastic evening, and one of those experiences that reminded me how small the world really is. Pablo's best friend was originally from Cyprus, which is where my good friend Andrea is from, and another friend was an American expat originally from Texas—and none of his friends believed that he had found me on the street, lost.

Later that evening, Pablo told me he had decided to talk to me and help me because he had watched *Waking Life* and was moved by a particular scene where a girl passes a stranger but then turns around and asks if they can start over and have real human interaction. You can watch the clip online if you search for "Waking Life—I Don't Want to Be an Ant."

desserts & baked goods

GLOBAL

almond cookies

SERVES 14

- 1¼ c white whole-wheat flour, divided
- 1 tbsp cornmeal
- 1 tsp baking powder
- ½ c raw sugar
- ¼ c unsweetened applesauce
- ½ c nondairy milk
- 1 tsp almond extract
- cinnamon, for dusting

Chef's Note For a less sweet cookie, reduce the sugar to ¼ or ⅓ c. You can also add a touch more almond extract for a more intense almond flavor.

The word "cookie" is mainly a North American term, used exclusively in the United States and some parts of Canada. What we know as a cookie is called a biscuit in Europe and most other areas of the world. Almond-flavored cookies . . . err, almond-flavored biscuits are a common offering in bakeries throughout Europe, and they're a traditional Chinese pastry too. A total sucker for almond extract, I knew I had to make almond biscuits when I returned home!

Preheat oven to 350°F. Line a cookie sheet with parchment paper or use a silicone mat, and set aside. In a large mixing bowl, whisk flour, cornmeal, baking powder, and a pinch of salt together. Then stir in sugar, applesauce, nondairy milk, and almond extract. The batter will be very sticky. Drop spoonfuls on your prepared cookie sheet, and use the back of the spoon to smooth the drops of batter into little circle medallions. Sprinkle cinnamon on top of each cookie and bake 7–10 minutes, or until firm to the touch and golden around the edges.

Chef's Note These cookies spread and expand during baking.

PER COOKIE | Calories 68, Total Fat 0.3g, Carbohydrates 15.5g, Fiber 1.2g, Sugars 8.0g, Protein 1.4g

anise cookies

ITALY

I grew up eating Italian anise cookies every year at Christmas. After seeing them again when I was in Italy, I came home and finally adapted my grandmother's recipe. If you're unfamiliar with anise, it tastes like black licorice.

Preheat oven to 350°F. Grease a cookie sheet or line with parchment paper and set aside. Whisk flour with cornstarch, baking soda, and a pinch of salt until combined. Add beans, anise extract, maple syrup, applesauce, and sugar (if using). Stir to combine—it might look dry at first, but keep combining. If dryness persists, add a splash of nondairy milk (when in doubt, wetter is better). Flour your hands and pick off 8 walnut-sized pieces of dough. Roll each into a ball, then flatten into mini "hockey puck" shapes. Bake 10–14 minutes, or until golden and firm to the touch (the cookies will puff up). Meanwhile, prepare icing by combining powdered sugar and nondairy milk to form a thick paste, adding anise extract one drop at a time (a little bit goes a long, long way!). Once cookies are done baking, allow to cool and then slather icing on top.

Chef's Note White whole-wheat or whole-wheat pastry flour may be substituted for the oat flour.

Chef's Note My grandmother also added little colored sprinkle balls to her cookies.

SERVES 8

- 1 c oat flour
- 1 tbsp cornstarch
- ½ tsp baking soda
- ¼ c white beans (any kind), mashed
- ½ tsp anise extract
- ¼ c maple syrup
- 1–2 tbsp raw sugar (optional)
- ¼ c unsweetened applesauce
- nondairy milk

ICING (MAKES ½ CUP)

- 1 c powdered sugar
- 5 tsp nondairy milk
- anise extract

Chef's Note Any white bean, such as cannellini, navy, or butter bean (cooked or canned), may be used in this recipe.

PER COOKIE | Calories 90, Total Fat 0.3g, Carbohydrates 20.2g, Fiber 2.1g, Sugars 7.1g, Protein 2.5g

blueberry bundt cake

PRONUNCIATION TIP
Bundkuchen sounds like "boondt-ku-hun" and *Gugelhupf* sounds like "google-hopf."

The English word "bundt" is derived from the German *Bundkuchen*, also called *Gugelhupf*, a ring-shaped cake originating in southern Germany, Austria, and Switzerland.

Preheat oven to 350°F. Grease a bundt pan and set aside. In a mixing bowl, combine flour, baking powder, baking soda, and sugar. Add nondairy milk and applesauce, then stir until just combined. Stir in blueberries. Pour batter into prepared pan and bake 25–40 minutes, until a toothpick inserted in the middle comes out clean. Meanwhile, make icing. In a small bowl, whisk powdered sugar with orange juice, zest, and nondairy milk as necessary until a runny glaze forms. Spoon glaze over warm cake and let run down the sides.

GERMANY

AUSTRIA

SWITZERLAND

SERVES 12

- 2 c white whole-wheat flour
- 1 tsp baking powder
- ½ tsp baking soda
- ½ c raw sugar
- 1 c nondairy milk
- ¼ c unsweetened applesauce
- 1 c frozen blueberries

ICING

- 1 c powdered sugar
- 1 tsp orange juice
- 1 tbsp orange zest
  nondairy milk, as needed

PER SERVING

PER SLICE (NO ICING) Calories 112, Total Fat 0.6g, Carbohydrates 25g, Fiber 2.4g, Sugars 10.7g, Protein 2.8g

ICING (PER TBSP) Calories 60, Total Fat 0g, Carbohydrates 15.2g, Fiber 0g, Sugars 14.7g, Protein 0g

Chef's Note If you don't have a bundt pan, a square 8- or 9-inch pan will work, but you will need to adjust baking time accordingly.

FRANCE

cherry clafoutis

■ ■ PRONUNCIATION TIP
The "s" is silent so the "i" is pronounced in *Clafoutis*; sounds like "cla-fou-tee."

SERVES 9

- ½ c white whole-wheat flour
- 1 tbsp cornstarch
- 6 oz silken tofu
- ½ tsp vanilla extract
- ½ tsp almond extract
- ¼ c nondairy milk, divided
- ½ c raw sugar
- 1¾ c red tart (pitted) cherries
- powdered sugar (optional)

Chef's Note I use a 14.5-oz can of red tart (pitted) cherries in water, not syrup, drained.

Chef's Note I don't grease my glass pie dish and my Clafoutis always lifts out fine when it's cool, but some of my testers had problems with it sticking. To prevent sticking, spritz an oil-spray can once, quickly, then use a paper towel to move the grease spray around the dish, creating a thin, shiny layer all around.

Cherry Clafoutis originated in the Limousin region of France and is a popular custard-like dessert with a slight pancake-like texture. When any fruits other than cherries are used (such as plums, prunes, or blackberries), the dish is called *flaugnarde*.

Preheat oven 375°F. In a mixing bowl, whisk flour with cornstarch. In a blender or food processor, puree tofu, extracts, and 1 tbsp nondairy milk until it's creamy like pudding. Pour tofu mixture into flour mixture and add raw sugar and cherries. Stir mixture a few strokes, until it's mostly combined. Then add remaining nondairy milk (3 tbsp) and stir a few more times, until completely combined. Pour into a shallow glass pie dish and bake 40–50 minutes, until golden and somewhat firm throughout, like pumpkin pie. When you touch the clafoutis, it should be soft but not mush—sponge-like. Allow to cool for 10–15 minutes. Clafoutis should be warm when served but not piping hot out of the oven. Garnish with a dusting of powdered sugar, if desired.

PER SERVING
(WITHOUT SUGAR DUSTING)

Calories 104, Total Fat 0.8g, Carbohydrates 22.5g, Fiber 1.4g, Sugars 16.3g, Protein 2.6g

chocolate glazed doughnuts

GLOBAL

I always thought doughnuts were an American food, but they are popular globally. You will find doughnuts or similar regional variations in Africa, Asia, Europe, North America, South America, the United Kingdom, Oceania, and the Middle East.

Preheat oven to 350°F. In a small bowl, whisk nondairy milk, lemon juice, maple syrup, light brown sugar, and vanilla until foamy and bubbly. In a large bowl, whisk flour, cocoa, salt, baking powder, baking soda, and chocolate chips (crushed). Pour the wet ingredients into the dry mix and use a spatula to combine. Spoon into a greased 6-doughnut pan. Bake for 15 minutes. Meanwhile, prepare the icing by whisking ingredients. Submerge cooked but cool doughnuts into icing and let glaze drip off. Transfer to a wire rack for drying.

SERVES 9

- 1 c nondairy milk
- 1 tsp lemon juice
- 3 tbsp pure maple syrup
- 2 tsp vanilla extract
- ¼ c packed light brown sugar
- 2 c whole-wheat pastry flour
- ¼ c unsweetened cocoa
- ½ tsp salt
- ½ tsp baking powder
- ½ tsp baking soda
- ¼ c vegan chocolate chips

ICING

- 1 c confectioner's sugar
- 1 tbsp pure maple syrup
- 1 tsp vanilla extract
- 1 tbsp nondairy milk

PER SERVING

WITHOUT ICING Calories 152, Total Fat 1.6g, Carbohydrates 30.9g, Fiber 3.7g, Sugars 9.1g, Protein 3.4g

WITH ICING Calories 213, Total Fat 1.6g, Carbohydrates 45.8g, Fiber 3.7g, Sugars 10.4g, Protein 3.4g

ENGLAND

bread pudding

Bread pudding is one of my parents' favorite desserts, and this is their recipe made vegan. I've always associated bread pudding with England, but it's also a popular dessert in Ireland, France, Belgium, Malta, and Argentina, among many other countries. If you're unfamiliar with bread pudding, it tastes a lot like French toast, only moister.

SERVES 6

- 3 c stale or toasted bread, cubed
- ½ c raisins (optional)
- ½ c raw sugar
- 2 c nondairy milk
- 3 oz silken tofu (about ⅓ c)
- ½ tsp vanilla extract
- ¼ c chickpea flour
- cinnamon, to taste

Place bread pieces in a square 8- or 9-inch glass casserole baking dish, then mix in raisins if using. In a blender, combine sugar, nondairy milk, tofu, vanilla, chickpea flour, and cinnamon, as desired (I use about ½ tsp) and blend until smooth and creamy. Pour tofu mixture over bread and raisins. Place casserole dish inside a pan with 1-inch hot water (from the tap is hot enough). Bake at 350°F 40–50 minutes, until it's somewhat firm to the touch and sort of pulls away from the pan if you stick a knife down the side of it. A little liquid is fine, but it shouldn't be soupy. Bread pudding also firms as it cools. Serve warm or cold.

PER SERVING | Calories 222, Total Fat 3.3g, Carbohydrates 40.1g, Fiber 4.7g, Sugars 20.1g, Protein 8.4g

date bread

IRAQ

I was first introduced to this Iraqi treat in Switzerland. I know what you're thinking—how is that possible? But the date bread was the vegan dessert of the day at a local vegetarian-friendly café I stopped at in Zurich. The dates give this bread a slight caramel taste. Yum!

Preheat oven to 350°F and grease a bread pan or use a nonstick pan. In a large mixing bowl, whisk flour with baking powder, baking soda, sugar, and several dashes of cinnamon, until well combined. Add applesauce, vanilla, and nuts (if using) and set aside. Place dates in a bowl and pour 1 c hot water over top. Let sit for a few minutes, then pour dates and water in to the flour mix. Stir until combined, then add 1 tbsp water and stir again. Transfer batter to your prepared pan and bake 50 minutes–1 hour—until it has risen and is crusty on the outside and firm through the center.

SERVES 12

- 2 c white whole-wheat flour
- 1 tsp baking powder
- ½ tsp baking soda
- ¾ c brown sugar
- ground cinnamon
- ⅓ c unsweetened applesauce
- 1 tsp vanilla extract
- 2 c chopped dates
- 1 c chopped walnuts (optional)

PER SLICE | Calories 189, Total Fat 0.5g, Carbohydrates 46.2g, Fiber 4.5g, Sugars 29.0g, Protein 3.4g

FRANCE

crêpes

Crêpes are thin French pancakes, and they are exceptionally popular throughout France. Crêpes can be served savory or sweet with any filling combination you can think of.

SERVES 6

1 c nondairy milk (approximate)

2 tbsp pure maple syrup

¼ tsp baking powder

1 c chickpea flour

1 tbsp sugar (optional, for sweet crêpes)

filling for crêpes

In a 2-c glass measuring cup, pour in ⅔ c nondairy milk, maple syrup, plus enough water so that the mixture levels off at the 1-c mark. Whisk in baking powder, chickpea flour, and sugar. Add another ⅓ c nondairy milk and whisk again. If the batter is really thick, you can add another 1–3 tbsp water, but you don't want it too runny or watery. Crêpe batter needs to be able to move around in the pan with ease when you swirl, but it should not be runny like water. Set batter aside temporarily and get your nonstick skillet hot. You'll know it's ready when a droplet of water fizzles. Reduce heat to medium, pull skillet off the burner, and pour in batter, enough to create a thin lining, swirling the batter around the skillet. Place the skillet back on the burner for about 30 seconds. Once a nonstick spatula goes under it easily, flip it over. The other side does not take long to cook, just a few seconds. Press down with the spatula, flip over to check it, then set it aside and make more crêpes. Add prepared fillings to the center of your crêpes and roll up like a burrito.

PER CRÊPE | Calories 145, Total Fat 2.5g, Carbohydrates 25.1g, Fiber 6.0g, Sugars 7.5g, Protein 6.6g

whole-wheat pizza dough

GREECE

Pizza has a rather colorful history. For starters, it was invented in Greece (true story!). The Greeks ate their flatbreads with toppings, and this culinary concept spread to Italy where the "pizza" we know today originated. Interestingly, cheese was not added to pizza until the late 1800s, so I guess all those cheeseless vegetable pizzas I ate in Italy were most authentic!

Stir yeast in 1 c warm water and let sit for 5 minutes, or until the water is a beige color. Meanwhile, combine flours, gluten, salt, and sugar. Make a well in center of your dry ingredients, pour yeast mixture in, and stir until it forms a ball of dough. Turn out onto a clean surface, lightly floured with cornmeal, and knead 5 minutes. The dough should be a smooth, elastic ball. Place in a glass or metal bowl and cover. Put it in a warm place, such as an unheated oven, and wait for it to double in size. It will take about an hour of resting for the dough to rise sufficiently. Punch the dough, reshape into a ball, and let it rise again.

Freeze or refrigerate if not using immediately (do not refrigerate for more than 24 hours). When ready to use, divide into 1, 2, or 4 equal portions and roll into a pizza shape. Add toppings and place on pizza stone, pizza pan, or cookie sheet lined with parchment paper. Bake for 5–10 minutes at 450°F.

SERVES 8

- 1 packet active yeast
- 1 c whole-wheat flour
- 2 c whole-wheat pastry flour
- 3 tbsp vital wheat gluten
- 1 tsp salt
- 1 tbsp raw sugar
- 1 tbsp cornmeal

Chef's Note Double or triple this recipe when you are making it and store leftovers in the freezer so you always have healthy whole-wheat pizza dough on hand.

PER SERVING

Calories 173, Total Fat 0.7g, Carbohydrates 35.5g, Fiber 3.4g, Sugars 1.6g, Protein 4.6g

BELGIUM

SERVES 4

1 c whole-wheat pastry flour

¼ tsp ground cinnamon

¼ tsp salt

2 tsp baking powder

nutmeg

1 c nondairy milk

¼ tsp vanilla

Chef's Note If your waffle iron is not a nonstick brand, you may need to lightly spritz it with oil spray.

Chef's Note Traditionally, waffles were served as a snack or dessert in Belgium; they are not eaten as a breakfast food with syrup like they are in America. Today, however, many of the cafés and street vendors in Belgium load Brussels waffles up with fresh fruit (i.e., strawberries and bananas), whipped cream, and chocolate sauce, a practice considered "unauthentic" by some locals but beloved by tourists.

courtney's waffles

Waffles are a Belgian specialty, and each part of the country has its own style. For example, what we know in America as the Belgian waffle is actually the Brussels waffle: a waffle that is rectangular in shape with a higher grid pattern that forms deep, square-shaped pockets. This is different from the Liège waffle, which is oval-shaped, sweeter, and a little bit crispy.

This is my sister's basic recipe for healthy waffles. They come out reminiscent of Brussels waffles, but we don't use yeast in the batter, which is a traditional ingredient in all Belgian waffles. (Baking powder, which we use, is specific to American-style waffle batter.)

In a mixing bowl, whisk together flour, cinnamon, salt, baking powder, and nutmeg until well combined. Add nondairy milk and vanilla, then mix well. Once the waffle iron is fully heated (mine has a light that goes off), pour in one-quarter of the batter and close lid. I find it is best to start pouring the batter in the center and work my way out; otherwise I use too much batter. When the light goes back off (or on, depending on your machine), the waffle is done. Repeat with remaining batter.

PER WAFFLE | Calories 124, Total Fat 1.3g, Carbohydrates 23.8g, Fiber 3.4g, Sugars 0g, Protein 3.3g

FRANCE

asparagus quiche

Other than a baguette, quiche is probably the most well-known French food outside of France. Here I've paired quiche with asparagus, which gives the quiche a great added texture.

SERVES 9

1 lb firm or extra-firm tofu

¼ c nutritional yeast

¼ c cornstarch

2 tbsp Dijon mustard

1 tbsp low-sodium soy sauce

1 tsp onion powder (granulated)

1 tsp garlic powder (granulated)

¼ tsp turmeric

¼ tsp black pepper

ground nutmeg

1 bunch green onions

1 bunch asparagus

PER SERVING

Calories 85, Total Fat 2.6g, Carbohydrates 10.1g, Fiber 3.3g, Sugars 1.9g, Protein 7.9g

Preheat oven to 350°F. Lightly grease a shallow 9-inch pie dish or line with parchment paper and set aside. In a food processor or blender, combine all ingredients listed from tofu through black pepper, with a few dashes of nutmeg, blending until smooth and creamy, stopping to scrape sides as necessary. Slice rooty bottom off green onions, then slice remaining onions and transfer to a mixing bowl. Cut woody bottom off asparagus (about bottom one-third) and slice remaining into ¼-inch pieces, reserving 6 or more half spears for garnish. Combine tofu mixture with green onions and sliced asparagus, until well mixed. Transfer batter to your prepared dish and spread around using a spatula so that it is even and packed down tight. Place asparagus spears on top like the spokes of a wheel (my friend LJ gets creative and makes a big peace sign!) Bake 30–40 minutes, until golden in color and center is firm, not mushy. Allow to cool for 10 minutes or to room temperature but slightly warm for best slicing.

Zurich has a certain way about it that makes it feel different from the rest of Europe. I felt very comfortable there, at home even, as though I'd lived there before. It just had this vibe . . . I can't really put my finger on it, a sort of "independence" attitude that made it stand apart from the rest of Europe.

My best friend Jim and I sat by the river talking for a long while (it was our last city together on my trip) and then dared to dip our feet in when we saw others swimming. Our toes lasted about 10 seconds. To say the water was cold would be a gross understatement. Those Swiss are brave.

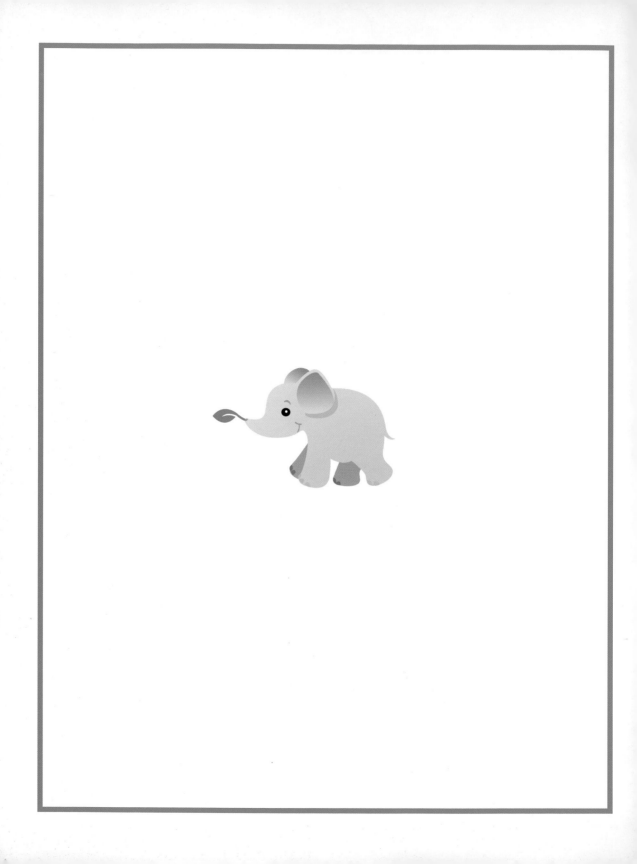

pasta, noodles, & sauce

ITALY

bolognese sauce

As the name suggests, Bolognese sauce (called *ragù alla bolognese* in Italian) originates in Bologna, Italy. I brought the original recipe, written in Italian, back with me from Italy and follow it pretty exactly, except that I use mushrooms instead of beef and nondairy milk. I have also added garlic and herbs, which are not in the traditional recipe, but I find they add more flavor to the sauce. Serve over pasta.

MAKES 3 CUPS

½ c carrots, chopped
½ c celery, chopped
½ c onion, chopped
    vegetable broth
8 oz brown mushrooms
½ c red wine
1 tbsp Italian seasoning
6 tbsp tomato paste, divided
1 14-oz can fire-roasted tomatoes
1 tsp dried oregano
2–4 tbsp nondairy milk

Chef's Note The original recipe takes about 5 hours to make. This version still takes about an hour, but it's well worth it and fairly passive.

Combine carrot, celery, and onion (*soffritto*) in a blender or food processor and process until it's well minced but not mushy or liquid (coarse). Line a large pot with a thin layer of vegetable broth and sauté *soffritto* until it has taken on a brown color and the liquid has totally evaporated, about 2–3 minutes. Meanwhile, remove stems from mushrooms (save for another use) and pulse mushrooms in a food processor or blender until fine and crumbly, like the consistency of ground beef. Transfer mushrooms to *soffritto*, stirring to combine. Add wine, then add 1 c water, enough so there is a thin layer on top of the mushrooms, about 1–2 c (it's better to add too much than too little). Whisk in Italian seasoning, 2 tbsp tomato paste, then cover, and bring to a boil.

Once boiling, remove cover and let boil, cooking off the liquid (reduce by at least half). Meanwhile, transfer tomatoes (with juices) to food processor or blender and puree until mostly smooth. Add to pot, stirring to combine. Continue to boil on high heat (uncovered) until liquid has greatly reduced, and the mixture is thick like pasta sauce and starts popping. At that point, cover and turn off heat. Stir in remaining tomato paste and oregano. Transfer half of the sauce, or as much as you like (some of my testers pureed everything and their kids didn't know they ate veggies!), to your blender and blend until smooth, or alternatively, leave it chunky. Return to pot, add 2–4 tbsp nondairy milk, stir, then season with salt and pepper.

Chef's Note Some of my testers had great success making this in a Crock-Pot. Combine all ingredients except the nondairy milk in the Crock-Pot and let it cook on low for 5 hours. Add the nondairy milk shortly before serving.

Chef's Note In Italy, Bolognese sauce is served with *tagliatelle*, a long, flat ribbon pasta similar to fettuccine. Elsewhere, Bolognese sauce is commonly served with spaghetti.

PER SERVING (¼ CUP)	Calories 35, Total Fat 0.5g, Carbohydrates 5.1g, Fiber 1.2g, Sugars 2.9g, Protein 1.39g

SPAIN

"cheater" romesco sauce

Don't let the name fool you: Romesco sauce comes from Catalonia, Spain, not Rome. Keeping with the traditional recipe, I do use a bit of almonds, making this a "cheater" recipe since it's not fat-free. Serve romesco sauce with grilled vegetables like zucchini or summer squash. In Barcelona, romesco sauce is frequently served with grilled or roasted asparagus.

MAKES ABOUT 1 CUP

- ¼ c vegetable broth
- 5 garlic cloves, minced
- ½ Spanish onion, diced
  red pepper flakes
- 1 12-oz jar roasted red bell peppers in water (3 peppers)
- 1–2 tbsp tomato paste
- ¼ c raw almonds
  smoked paprika

Chef's Note If your romesco sauce is acidic, add a little sugar.

Line a medium pot with a thin layer of broth and sauté garlic, onion, and a dash or two red pepper flakes over high heat until onions are translucent, garlic is golden, and the liquid has evaporated. Transfer the onion–garlic mixture to a blender and set aside momentarily. Pour a little water (or broth) into the pot to deglaze the bottom, using a spatula to loosen any bits, then pour that mixture into the blender. Add bell peppers, 1 tbsp tomato paste, and almonds, and whiz until smooth and creamy. The mixture should look orangey. Return sauce to your pot and heat over low until warm. Taste, adding more tomato paste if desired and several dashes of smoked paprika (about ¼ tsp or more), and stir to combine. Season with salt and pepper and serve.

PER SERVING
(ABOUT ¼ CUP, 4 SERVINGS TOTAL)

Calories 72, Total Fat 3.2g, Carbohydrates 10.1g, Fiber 2.2g, Sugars 5.1g, Protein 2.6g

vodka sauce

ITALY

Penne alla vodka is one of Italy's best-known dishes. The main ingredient, vodka sauce, is a smooth, tomato-based sauce cooked with vodka, cream, and fresh Italian herbs. The vodka's function is to release and heighten flavors in the tomato that are normally inaccessible. Some flavors in tomatoes are alcohol-soluble, meaning they will be released only if alcohol is involved. Maybe now you appreciate why Italians love to cook with wine and spirits!

Line a saucepan with a thin layer of broth and sauté garlic, plus a shake or two red pepper flakes, over high heat until garlic is golden but not burned, and the liquid has evaporated. Stir in tomato sauce and vodka. Bring to a near boil, then reduce to medium and let simmer uncovered on low heat, until the vodka cooks off and the liquid reduces—about 10 minutes. Meanwhile, combine tofu, basil, and non-dairy milk in a blender, and puree until smooth and creamy. Once tomato–vodka mixture is done, add to blender and puree again until everything is smooth, creamy, and pink in color. Return vodka sauce to saucepan and warm over very low heat, adding salt if desired. Turn off heat, cover, and let rest for 10 minutes (or longer if you can). The flavors will intensify as it sits, and the sauce will take on a pinker hue with time.

MAKES 1¼ CUP

- ¼ c vegetable broth
- ½–1 tbsp minced garlic
  red pepper flakes
- 1 15-oz can tomato
  sauce
- ¼ c vodka (yes!)
- ¼ c silken tofu
- ¼ c fresh basil, packed
- 2 tbsp nondairy milk

Chef's Note I prefer to use sweetened nondairy milk in this recipe.

PER SERVING (¼ CUP) | Calories 89, Total Fat 0.4g, Carbohydrates 7.6g, Fiber 1.4g, Sugars 4.3g, Protein 2.2g

spaghetti alla puttanesca

ITALY

Spaghetti alla puttanesca is one of the lesser-known dishes in Italian cuisine but one of my personal favorites. It's easy to make and sure to impress! Although it's traditionally made with spaghetti, I love it with linguine.

Cook pasta according to package instructions. Drain and, while pasta is still warm, mix with Olive Tapenade. Garnish with fresh parsley and serve.

SERVES 2

4 oz whole-wheat spaghetti or linguine

Olive Tapenade (p. 206)

fresh parsley, minced (garnish)

PER SERVING | Calories 121, Total Fat 4.0g, Carbohydrates 19.7g, Fiber 0.7g, Sugars 1.5g, Protein 4.0g

Chef's Note For a gluten-free option, use brown rice, spaghetti, or linguine.

ITALY

gin's gnocchi

From my good friend Gin: "This is a fairly basic recipe that my family brought over from Italy. It is one of the very few family recipes my grandfather taught me."

SERVES 4

- 3 large russet potatoes
- 1½ c whole-wheat pastry flour
- 2 tbsp dried basil
- 2 tbsp dried oregano
- 1 tsp salt
- ½ tsp garlic powder (granulated)
- ½ tsp onion powder (granulated)
- nondairy milk

Chef's Note Gin says: "In my experience, any flour should work but grainier flour will make grainier gnocchi."

Preheat oven to 350°F. Bake potatoes in oven, placing them directly on the rack (do not wrap the potatoes in foil!). It takes at least 40 minutes but up to 1 hour for the potatoes to cook fully. While the potatoes are baking, mix flour, dried herbs, salt, and seasonings in a large mixing bowl, making a well in the middle of the mix. Once the potatoes are done, peel the skins off (it should be very easy at this point). Place the potatoes in a separate bowl and mash until there are no lumps, adding 1 tsp nondairy milk at a time, as needed, but do not exceed 2 tbsp total. Put the potatoes in blender or food processor if necessary, as it is very important that your mashed potatoes are smooth and thick, not runny.

Add mashed potatoes to the flour mixture and mix with your hands, kneading it like bread dough. Once the ingredients are mixed well, form "dough" into a ball. Set aside and bring a pot of heavily salted water to a boil on the stove.

Flour the counter and pick off a chunk of the mixture, rolling it into another ball and then rolling it out into a "snake" on the floured counter. Cut the snake into piece approximately ½ inch in size. Form

the pieces into ovals and pinch the pointed end. (It will look a little bit like a pillow.) Pull a fork across the back rounded part to give it that signature gnocchi shape—essentially give it stripes. Repeat with remaining potato "dough."

Drop gnocchi in batches in the boiling water. When gnocchi floats to the surface, it's done. Spoon gnocchi out and place in a bowl in the oven to keep warm while the rest are cooking. Top gnocchi with your fave pasta sauce and garnish with parsley.

PER SERVING | Calories 365, Total Fat 1.3g, Carbohydrates 78.5g, Fiber 12.2g, Sugars 3.5g, Protein 9.5g

ITALY

pasta e fagioli

PRONUNCIATION TIP
Fagioli sounds like "fah-joe-lee."

Pasta e fagioli, or *pasta fazool* as it's often called in the United States, is one of a few Italian dishes that is traditionally vegetarian. The name literally means pasta and beans, and although modern variations (especially those outside of Italy) often contain sausage or other meats, *pasta e fagioli* was traditionally composed of just three ingredients: tomato sauce, pasta, and beans. Although any pasta or white bean will do here, cannellini beans and small-shaped pasta such as elbow macaroni make for the most authentic experience.

SERVES 4

- 6 oz whole-wheat or gluten-free pasta
- 1 15-oz can white beans (any kind), drained and rinsed
- 2½ c marinara sauce
- fresh basil (optional garnish)
- vegan Parmesan cheese (optional garnish)

Cook pasta according to package directions. Just before the pasta is done, add beans to the boiling water, so they warm up. (It only takes about a minute.) Drain off water and return beans and pasta to the pot. Add warmed marinara, stirring to combine. Garnish with fresh basil or vegan Parmesan cheese, if desired.

PER SERVING | Calories 284, Total Fat 3.1g, Carbohydrates 53.3g, Fiber 8.8g, Sugars 7.7g, Protein 11.2g

ITALY

lasagna

Lasagna is perhaps the most beloved Italian dish outside of Italy, and for good reason: It's delicious, relatively easy to prepare, and an all-around crowd pleaser.

Preheat oven to 350°F. Cook frozen spinach according to package instructions, then press out excess water and set aside. Prepare Tofu Ricotta and mix spinach into it, and set the mixture aside. Cook pasta al dente according to package instructions and immediately rinse with cold water, then pat dry with a clean kitchen towel. Spread a very thin layer of marinara sauce on the bottom of a square 9×9 glass casserole dish. Place 5 noodles side by side, covering the bottom. Spread half of the Tofu Ricotta on the noodles, then spoon a little marinara on top. Place mushrooms on top of the Tofu Ricotta layer. Place 5 more noodles side by side on top, and spoon marinara on top. Add remaining Tofu Ricotta and then add another layer of noodles. Spoon remaining marinara on top of Tofu Ricotta. (You will likely have leftover marinara.) Bake uncovered 30–35 minutes, until noodles start to get crisp at the edges.

SERVES 4

- 10 oz frozen spinach
  Tofu Ricotta (p. 204)
- 15 whole-wheat or brown rice lasagna noodles
- 2 28 oz jars marinara sauce
- 1 c mushrooms, sliced

Chef's Note You can use brown (cremini) or white mushrooms in this recipe.

Chef's Note Lasagna is referred to as "lasagne" in Italy. "Lasagne" is the plural form, meaning more than one lasagna ribbon is used in the dish. The Italian plural forms of most other types of pasta also end in "e." ("Lasagna" actually refers to one single pasta ribbon.)

PER SERVING | Calories 378, Total Fat 5.1g, Carbohydrates 76.2g, Fiber 13.3g, Sugars 16.4g, Protein 16.6g

THAILAND

"cheater" pad thai

When writing this cookbook I asked my fans (called "Herbies") what their favorite international recipe was from my previous cookbooks. This Pad Thai was the hands-down favorite. I call this "cheater" pad thai because it's ridiculously easy and quick to make and also because it uses 1 tbsp of peanut butter, so it's not fat-free.

SERVES 2

- ¼ lb thick rice noodles
- 2 tbsp low-sodium soy sauce
- 1 tbsp smooth peanut butter
- 1 tbsp sweet red chili sauce
- ¼ tsp granulated garlic powder
- ¼ tsp ground ginger
- ¼ tsp hot sauce
- 3 oz bean sprouts
- chopped raw peanuts (optional garnish)
- lime wedge (optional garnish)

Prepare rice noodles according to package directions. In a small bowl, whisk 2 tbsp warm water, soy sauce, peanut butter, chili sauce, garlic powder, ginger, and hot sauce together until combined. It may appear too runny at first, but it's not. Taste, adding more hot sauce if desired. Using tongs, toss prepared noodles with sauce until all noodles are evenly coated. Plate and top with bean sprouts. Garnish with chopped raw peanuts and a lime wedge if desired.

Chef's Note For a gluten-free version, use wheat-free tamari in place of the soy sauce

PER SERVING
("CHEATER" PAD THAI)

Calories 283, Total Fat 4.3g, Carbohydrates 55.0g, Fiber 2.7g, Sugars 4.1g, Protein 7.9g

LOWER-CALORIE PAD THAI

✓ QUICK ✓ GLUTEN-FREE

For a lower-carbohydrate and lower-calorie pad
Thai, substitute 2 c thinly sliced blanched
cabbage for half of the rice noodles.

VEGETABLE PAD THAI

✓ QUICK ✓ GLUTEN-FREE

Double the sauce. Cook one 15-oz package of frozen
stir-fry veggies according to package instructions
and toss with sauce and noodles.

SWEDEN

swedish "meatballs"

My husband is part Swedish, and Swedish meatballs (called *Svenska kóttbullar* in Swedish) are one of the few Swedish foods he grew up eating. This is a vegan version of Ikea's recipe with tempeh standing in for meatballs.

SERVES 2

1 8-oz package tempeh, cubed

low-sodium soy sauce

GRAVY

1 tbsp low-sodium soy sauce

1 tbsp nutritional yeast

2 tbsp Vegan Worcestershire Sauce (pg. 237)

1 tsp onion powder (granulated)

1 tsp garlic powder (granulated)

allspice

nutmeg

¼ c nondairy milk

3 tbsp white whole-wheat flour

1–3 tsp raspberry jam

cooked brown rice

minced parsley (optional garnish)

Bring a pot of water to a boil, then add tempeh plus a splash of soy sauce and boil tempeh for 10 minutes. Drain off water and set warm tempeh aside. In the same pot, whisk 1 c water with soy sauce, nutritional yeast, Vegan Worcestershire Sauce, onion powder, garlic powder, a light dash of allspice, a slightly heavier dash of nutmeg, nondairy milk, flour, and 1 tsp jam until well combined. Cook over medium heat, whisking regularly until warm and gravy-thick. Taste, adding more jam as desired plus salt and white pepper. Mix tempeh with gravy until well coated, then serve over a bed of rice, garnished with parsley.

PER SERVING Calories 306, Total Fat 5.5g, Carbohydrates 47.1g, Fiber 11.4g, Sugars 4.0g, Protein 21.8g

Chef's Note Lingonberry jam is traditionally used in this recipe, but it's nearly impossible to come across in the United States, so I use seedless raspberry jam as a substitute. Red currant or strawberry jam would also work, though raspberry is much better.

no-meat "meatballs"

Although meatballs are often associated with Italian cuisine in America, they are actually a traditional dish in more than 20 different countries. The base ingredients of meatballs are generally the same globally—it is how or what they are served with that is different. For example, in Japan, they are served with ketchup and Worcestershire sauce; and in Romania, they are deep-fried...just to name a few!

Preheat oven to 350°F. Line cookie sheet with parchment paper and set aside. Mash kidney beans with a fork in a mixing bowl until mostly pureed with some half beans and bean parts remaining, then set aside. Pulse onion and garlic cloves in a food processor until minced and transfer to mixing bowl. Repeat with carrot and transfer to mixing bowl. Pulse or grind brown rice so that it is coarsely chopped, and transfer to your mixing bowl. Add ketchup, steak sauce, soy sauce, Dijon mustard, Italian seasoning, Vegan Worcestershire Sauce, and a few dashes of hot sauce, stirring to combine. Stir in oats. Use your hands to shape into walnut-size meatballs. Bake 20–30 minutes or until the meatballs are golden brown on the outside. Let cool 10–15 minutes—they firm as they cool.

MAKES 16

- 1 15-oz can kidney beans, drained and rinsed
- ¼ onion
- 2 garlic cloves
- 1 carrot, skinned
- 1 c cooked brown rice
- 2 tbsp ketchup
- 2 tbsp steak sauce
- 1–2 tbsp low-sodium soy sauce
- 1 tbsp Dijon mustard
- 1 tbsp Italian seasoning
- 1½ tsp Vegan Worcestershire Sauce (pg. 237)
- hot sauce, to taste
- ¾ c instant oats

Chef's Note If you do not have instant oats, pulse rolled oats in food processor to chew them up a bit.

PER SERVING (1 MEATBALL) | Calories 81, Total Fat 0.8g, Carbohydrates 15.8g, Fiber 2.7g, Sugars 1.3g, Protein 3g

ITALY

quick pesto

This pesto sauce comes together in an instant and is great for tired weeknights when the only thing you're capable of doing is boiling pasta.

MAKES 1½ CUPS

6 oz plain vegan yogurt

1 c fresh basil leaves, packed tight

1 garlic clove

1 lemon wedge (juice)

Variation Substitute 2 c fresh baby spinach for the basil, but you'll want to add more garlic.

Chef's Note If you can't find commercial vegan yogurt, try using 1 c soft or silken tofu.

Chef's Note The more basil, the merrier—you really want to pack your measuring cup full.

Combine yogurt, basil, and garlic in a blender or food processor and puree until smooth, creamy, and a brilliant green. Taste. If the yogurt was sweetened and the pesto is a little sweet for your taste, add about ¼ tsp lemon juice. You can also add more basil if the pesto is not as strong as you'd like. Add salt and pepper to taste. Toss ¼ c pesto with cooked pasta (slightly warm or lightly chilled but not piping hot), adding more pesto as necessary until the pasta is well coated, or use the pesto as a sandwich spread, as a pizza sauce, a dip, or any way you enjoy pesto.

PER SERVING (¼ CUP) | Calories 20, Total Fat 0.5g, Carbohydrates 2.3g, Fiber 0g, Sugars 2g, Protein 1.7g

PER SERVING (¼ CUP, SPINACH VARIATION) | Calories 16, Total Fat 0.4g, Carbohydrates 1.9g, Fiber 0g, Sugars 1.5g, Protein 1.4g

opg Blažević

opg Blažević

Rijeka, Croatia (2011)

Dijeka, Croatia (2011)

Some people gawk at designer cupcakes and cookies. I lose it for fruit stands. The fresh market in Croatia made my heart sing. I gorged myself on fruit I had never seen before, plus carrots, cucumbers, and tomatoes that were so vibrant in color I could not resist eating them in the middle of the street.

Mouth full of food, I said to my husband, "Can we just stay here? I feel so inspired. I want to write my entire cookbook with access to this market!" It really was a dream.

Barcelona, Spain (2011)

Then we went to Venice, where I was really blown away—farmer's market on a BOAT! Now that's what I'm talking about!

Perhaps the most famous European market is Barcelona's fresh market *La Boqueria*, which shames any other fresh market anywhere (see photos above). The pictures don't even come close to bringing it justice. Every kind of legume, mushroom, fruit, vegetable, and candy exists there . . . and in all their brilliance.

Many of my meals in Europe were fresh produce feasts. I once passed a man selling grapes in a wheelbarrow in Austria and was so enticed I ate a pile of grapes for lunch. Then in Italy, I bought so many cherries at a produce stand that I ate them for dinner and still had more for breakfast the next day. Another time, I carried apples, plums, and other fruits in my shirt all the way back to my hostel because I didn't have a bag and could not pass up the produce.

Europe's fresh markets also remind me of my life back in New York City, where I often decided what to have for dinner based on whatever I bought at the farmer's stand on the way home. I look forward to these markets and produce stands every time I return to Europe—and to the spontaneity of letting the produce decide what I'm having as my next meal.

Venice, Italy (2011)

gravies, condiments, sauces, & toppers

curry ketchup

GERMANY

I met up with a Herbie in Hamburg, and she took me to a local bar that had a special vegan menu. Having seen *currywurst* all over Germany (it's a popular fast food there), I decided to order the vegan *currywurst*. As soon as I ordered it, the waiter turned to me and said, "You know this is vegan—no meat, no nothing?" It took all I had not to burst out laughing. I nodded and said, "ja!" and as soon as he rounded the corner, Dorothee and I started laughing hysterically. Yes, we know it's vegan and without meat— that's why we wanted it! Nevertheless, the *currywurst* was delicious, but it was the sauce that really got my attention. I started asking around about how to make it and learned it was a fairly simple German recipe: curry powder, ketchup, and a few other spices. It's so simple yet so awesome!

Whisk ketchup, ½ tsp curry, onion powder, a dash of paprika, and a dash of cayenne together in a microwave-safe bowl. Microwave 15–30 seconds, until ketchup is warm. (If you don't have a microwave, you can gently warm it in a pot on the stovetop, stirring constantly on low.) Heating the mixture helps the ketchup lose some of its sweet taste while also helping the curry flavor blend in better. Once it's warm, whisk again and taste, adding another ¼ tsp curry powder if desired.

SERVES 4

¼ c ketchup

½–¾ tsp mild curry powder

onion powder (granulated)

paprika (sweet/ Hungarian)

cayenne pepper (optional)

Chef's Note If the ketchup is too thick, you can thin it out with a tiny bit of water or tomato sauce.

PER SERVING (1 TBSP) | Calories 21, Total Fat 0.0g, Carbohydrates 5.2g, Fiber 0g, Sugars 4.0g, Protein 0.1g

FRANCE

creamy dijon gravy

■ ■ **PRONUNCIATION TIP**
In French, the "H" is silent; it sounds like "oo-llandaise."

SERVES 4

- 1–2 tbsp Dijon mustard
- 1 15-oz can white beans (any kind), drained and rinsed
- ¾ c vegetable broth
- 1 tbsp nutritional yeast
- 1 tsp rubbed sage (not powdered)
- ½ tsp onion powder (granulated)
- ½ tsp garlic powder (granulated)

Chef's Note Any white bean, such as cannellini, navy, or butter beans, works in this recipe.

This thick gravy reminds me of a tangy Hollandaise sauce, so I love smothering asparagus or green beans with it.

Combine all ingredients in a blender and puree until smooth and creamy. Transfer to a saucepan and heat over low. Once warm, taste, adding more Dijon if desired, plus salt and pepper to taste.

Chef's Note Don't be fooled by the name; Hollandaise sauce is not from Holland. Rather, it's one of the five sauces central to French cuisine.

PER SERVING
(APPROXIMATELY ¼ CUP)

Calories 87, Fat 0.3g, Carbohydrates 18.4g, Fiber 7g, Sugars 0g, Protein 6.6g

MEXICO

pineapple & black bean salsa

MAKES 2½ CUPS

- 1 15-oz can black beans, drained and rinsed
- 1 bell pepper, diced
- ½ cucumber, diced
- 3–5 green onions, sliced
- ⅓ c cilantro, chopped
- 1 small lime (juice)
- 2–3 tbsp pineapple juice
- ½ c crushed pineapple
- ½ tsp chili powder
- ¼ tsp ground cumin
- 1–2 tsp hot sauce
- whole cilantro leaves (garnish)

The great thing about this recipe is how versatile it is—with slight adjustments you can make it spicy, tropical, or citrus-based. It's great as a salsa, a dip for corn chips, or a condiment like pico de gallo. You can also add diced avocado and corn if desired.

Combine all ingredients together and chill until serving. Garnish with a few whole cilantro leaves.

VARIATIONS:

Add more lime juice for a lime-based salsa, more pineapple juice or pineapple for a pineapple/tropical salsa, or minced jalapeño for a spicy kick.

Chef's Note This recipe is very forgiving. You can use white or red onions in place of the green onions, any color bell pepper, and so on.

Chef's Note If using no-salt or low-sodium beans, you might want to add ½ tsp soy sauce or salt to taste for a soy-free option.

PER SERVING (APPROXIMATELY ¼ C) | Calories 78, Fat 0.7g, Carbohydrates 14.6g, Fiber 4.6g, Sugars 2.8g, Protein 4.4g

hummus

**MIDDLE EAST
PALESTINE/ISRAEL**

We use hummus on everything at home: on top of a salad for protein and flavor, on a sandwich instead of mayo, with celery or carrots for a healthy snack, and so on. Here is my fat-free, homemade version. It's a base recipe, so you can create additional flavors by adding ingredients like olives, sun-dried tomatoes, fresh garlic, and so on.

In a blender or food processor, combine chickpeas, lemon juice, cumin, coriander, garlic powder, mustard, and miso (if using). Allow the motor to run until the beans are chopped up. Stop, scrape the sides, and add 1 tbsp broth. Allow the motor to run again, adding more broth as necessary, until the mixture achieves a smooth, hummus consistency. (I typically use 3½ tbsp broth.) You may need to stop and scrape the sides periodically. Once consistency is achieved, taste, adding more lemon or Dijon if desired (a little goes a long way!).

MAKES ABOUT 1 CUP

- 1 15-oz can chickpeas, drained and rinsed
- ½ small lemon (juice)
- ½ tsp ground cumin
- ½ tsp coriander
- ¼ tsp garlic powder (granulated)
- 1 tsp Dijon mustard
- ¼ tsp miso paste (optional)
- vegetable broth, as needed

PER SERVING
(APPROXIMATELY 1 TBSP)

Calories 21, Fat 0.2g, Carbohydrates 3.3g, Fiber 0.8g, Sugars 0g, Protein 1.1g

Vegan sandwich (with hummus) that I had at a vegan shop in Berlin, Germany (2011).

195

INDONESIA

"cheater" tofu satay

SERVES 2

1 lb extra-firm tofu, cut into triangles

SATAY SAUCE

1 tbsp peanut butter

1 tbsp lite coconut milk

1 tsp low-sodium soy sauce

ground ginger

garlic powder (granulated)

2–3 tsp sweet red chili sauce

hot sauce (optional)

Chef's Note Any plain nondairy milk may be substituted for the lite coconut milk.

Chef's Note For a gluten-free option, use wheat-free tamari in place of the soy sauce.

Satay is a national dish in Indonesia (where it originates), though it is also popular in several other Southeast Asian countries, such as Malaysia, Thailand, and the Philippines. In culinary terms, *satay* refers to skewered meat that's been grilled and then served with a peanut sauce. I am using tofu instead of meat, but the sauce (the best part!) remains the same. I call this a "cheater" recipe because I'm using a dab of peanut butter and a little bit of coconut milk, so this recipe is not fat-free.

Whisk peanut butter (smooth or crunchy) with coconut milk, soy sauce, a few dashes of ground ginger, a few dashes of garlic powder, and 2 tsp chili sauce until well combined. Taste, adding another 1 tsp red chili sauce if desired. For a spicier satay sauce, add hot sauce, such as sriracha, to taste. If the sauce is too thick, thin it out with extra coconut milk or nondairy milk.

Chef's Note For a truly authentic experience, you'll need to skewer and grill your tofu, but I often skip that step and just eat my tofu plain, dipped in the sauce.

PER SERVING | Calories 270, Total Fat 17.6g, Carbohydrates 8.8g, Fiber 1.4g, Sugars 4.0g, Protein 24.7g

chermoula (MOROCCAN PESTO)

MOROCCO

PRONUNCIATION TIP *Chermoula* sounds like "chehr-moo-lah."

This pesto is often used as a condiment in Moroccan cuisine. I like it spread on crackers and bread or mixed with chickpeas and couscous as a meal.

In a food processor or blender, combine garlic, cilantro, parsley, cumin, coriander, ¼ tsp paprika, a dash cayenne, lemon zest, lemon juice, salt, and ¼ c broth and process until thick and paste-like, stopping to scrape the sides as necessary. If it's not pureed into a paste, add another 1–2 tbsp broth as necessary to achieve the proper consistency. Then taste, adding more garlic, cilantro, parsley, lemon, paprika, salt, or cayenne if desired.

SERVES 2

- 2 garlic cloves, minced
- 1 c cilantro, packed tight
- ⅓ c parsley, packed tight
- ¼ tsp ground cumin
- ½ tsp ground coriander
- ¼–½ tsp smoked paprika
  cayenne pepper
  lemon zest
- 2 lemon wedges (juice)
- 4–6 tbsp vegetable broth

PER SERVING
(¼ CUP)

Calories 16, Total Fat 0.3g, Carbohydrates 3.4g, Fiber 1.0g, Sugars 0.6g, Protein 0.8g

197

MEXICO

quick queso

It's okay to go at this sauce with a spoon. I won't judge. It's also great with nachos, burritos, enchiladas, or inside a black bean quesadilla.

MAKES 1 CUP

- 1 c nondairy milk
- ⅓ c nutritional yeast
- 2 tbsp whole-wheat flour
- 1 tsp onion powder (granulated)
- 1 tsp garlic powder (granulated)
- ½ tsp ground cumin
- ¼ tsp paprika
- ¼ tsp chili powder or cayenne (optional)
- ¼–⅓ c salsa

Whisk all ingredients together in a saucepan. Bring to a boil over medium heat, stirring often until thick. Then stir in salsa (the queso takes on a bit of an orange coloring) and serve immediately.

PER SERVING [¼ CUP]
Calories 45, Total Fat 0.8g, Carbohydrates 6.2g, Fiber 1.6g, Sugars 1.8g, Protein 4.0g

enchilada sauce

MEXICO

The secret to making authentic enchilada sauce is the addition of cocoa. Once you've had homemade, you'll never buy enchilada sauce in a can again.

Whisk flour, cocoa, and spices together in a medium saucepan without heat. Add ¼ c broth and stir into a paste. Slowly whisk in remaining broth plus 1 c water. Bring to a boil over medium heat and whisk in tomato sauce. Allow to cook for a few minutes until it thickens slightly to the consistency of tomato soup. Remove from heat and add salt to taste, if necessary.

SERVES 4 CUPS

- 2 tbsp white whole-wheat or other flour
- 1 tsp unsweetened cocoa
- 2 tbsp chili powder
- 1 tsp dried oregano or marjoram
- 1 tsp ground cumin
- ½ tsp garlic powder (granulated)
- 2 c vegetable broth, divided
- 1 8-oz can tomato sauce

PER SERVING (¼ CUP) | Calories 13, Total Fat 0.3g, Carbohydrates 2.8g, Fiber 0.7g, Sugars 0.8g, Protein 0.5g

MEXICO

aj's pico de gallo

When I visited Mexico for the first time, I ordered a side of *pico* and the waiter corrected me, saying, "Mexican salsa?" Over the course of my trip, I realized what I knew as *pico de gallo* in the United States was simply known as Mexican salsa in Mexico. This recipe was developed by my friend Chef AJ, and it tastes exactly like what I had in Puerto Vallarta!

SERVES 2

- 3 Roma tomatoes (firm)
- 1 key lime
- 1 shallot
- 2 garlic cloves
- 1 jalapeño pepper
- cilantro, chopped (to taste)

Chef's Note Use a small lime (walnut-sized) rather than a larger one.

Cut tomatoes in half, squeeze out extra juice and seeds, and then dice. Place diced tomatoes in a bowl and add juice from the key lime. Dice or mince the shallot and garlic and add to the tomatoes. Finely dice the jalapeño, removing the seeds if you would like it less hot, and add it to the mixture. Add cilantro, season with black pepper, and stir to combine.

Chef's Note One of my favorite snacks in Mexico was a baked potato topped with fresh pico . . . er, Mexican salsa and lime juice. They love key limes in Mexico!

PER SERVING | Calories 64, Total Fat 0.5g, Carbohydrates 15.5g, Fiber 3.4g, Sugars 5.7g, Protein 2.6g

tofu feta

GREECE

I made this "cheese" a few years ago when a friend asked if you could make feta out of tofu (what a great idea!). You can also add this feta to Mama D's Spanakorizo (p. 120), which is how my friend Andrea's mom (from Cyprus) serves it.

Break tofu into a few large pieces in a mixing bowl and set aside. Whisk together all remaining ingredients, except nutritional yeast. Pour over tofu and mix with your hands, crumbling the tofu into smaller pieces as you go. Let rest for 10 minutes. Sprinkle 1 tbsp nutritional yeast over top and mix. Taste, adding more nutritional yeast if desired. This feta gets more flavorful as it ages.

MAKES ABOUT 2 CUPS

- 1 lb extra-firm tofu
- 2 tbsp water
- 4 tsp yellow miso
- ¼ c red wine vinegar
- 1 tbsp lemon juice
- 2 tsp dried basil
- 1 tsp dried oregano
- ¼ tsp dried rosemary
- 1–2 tbsp nutritional yeast

PER SERVING (¼ CUP) | Calories 69, Total Fat 3.6g, Carbohydrates 3.3g, Fiber 1.1, Sugars 1.0g, Protein 7.0g

Chef's Note For the best "feta" consistency, press tofu, freeze it overnight, and then let thaw before making the feta.

203

ITALY

tofu ricotta

I love this ricotta for my salads, but it also really jazzes up a plain bowl of pasta with marinara while adding a good bit of protein to a usually carb-heavy dish.

MAKES 2 CUPS

- 1 lb extra-firm tofu
- ¼ c nutritional yeast
- ½ tsp yellow or white miso (optional)
- 1 tsp lemon juice
- 1 tbsp Italian seasoning
- ¼ tsp onion powder (granulated)
- ¼ tsp garlic powder (granulated)

Give tofu a good squeeze, pressing out any excess moisture, then crumble into a mixing bowl using your hands. Add remaining ingredients and stir with a fork or your hands until well combined. Taste, adding another 1 tablespoon of nutritional yeast if desired, plus more miso, lemon juice, or Italian seasoning to taste. Add fresh black pepper and serve.

PER SERVING
(¼ CUP)

Calories 25, Total Fat 0.8g,
Carbohydrates 2.8g,
Fiber 1.3g, Sugars 0g,
Protein 2.5g

FRANCE

olive tapenade

Tapenade is a popular appetizer in the South of France, originating in Provençal. Traditionally, tapenade is prepared in a mortar and pestle, but I cheat and use my mini food processor. Spread tapenade on crackers, crusty French bread, or crudités.

MAKES 5 TBSP

- 1 garlic clove
- ½ c pitted kalamata olives (in water, not oil)
- 2 tsp capers
- 1 tbsp tomato paste
- dried oregano
- red pepper flakes
- low-sodium soy sauce (optional)
- vegetable broth, as needed

Place garlic, olives, capers, tomato paste, a pinch of oregano, and a pinch of red pepper flakes in blender or food processor. Add a light drizzle of soy sauce (if using) and blend. Add a splash of wine, water, or broth if necessary to reach a paste consistency.

PER SERVING (1 TBSP)   Calories 20, Total Fat 1.5g, Carbohydrates 1.9g, Fiber 0.7g, Sugars 0g, Protein 0.4g

Chef's Note Make ahead if possible. I find this tapenade tastes even better the next day.

quick mole sauce

MEXICO

Mole sauce was one of those things I always resisted, but when I finally gave it a try at a restaurant, I was hooked! Mole sauce is awesome! This recipe streamlines the authentic recipe, but the taste is spot on. I like to smother baked tofu with it, but it is most commonly used as an alternative to enchilada sauce.

Combine tomato sauce, cocoa, raisins, chili powder, onion powder, cinnamon, oregano, cumin, and a pinch of red pepper flakes together in a blender and whiz until thick and smooth and no raisin chunks remain (you may need to stop and scrape the sides). Thin out with a little water or broth as desired.

Heat gently in a saucepan over low heat until warm.

MAKES 2 CUPS

- 1 16-oz can tomato sauce
- ¼ c unsweetened cocoa
- ¼ c raisins
- 2¼ tsp chili powder
- 1 tsp onion powder (granulated)
- ½ tsp ground cinnamon
- ½ tsp dried oregano
- ½ tsp ground cumin
- red pepper flakes
- vegetable broth, as needed

PER SERVING (¼ CUP) | Calories 35, Total Fat 0.5g, Carbohydrates 8.6g, Fiber 2.0g, Sugars 5.3g, Protein 1.5g

Cinque de Terre, Italy (2006)

Gibraltar (2006)

When I was a sophomore in college, I struggled, as many students do, trying to pick my major. I'm the kind of person who does better with limits rather than having limitless options. All of the choices overwhelmed me, and the weight of the decisions became heavier with each passing day. What if I picked a major I ended up disliking? What if I picked a major that sent me down the wrong career path? Or what if I picked a major that wouldn't be strong in the job market? What if? What if? What if?

The day before I needed to declare my major, a postcard arrived in the mail. It depicted two Greek deities, with an inscription in Greek, and it had arrived from Greece. The message said "Greetings from the Place Chosen by the Gods," and that afternoon, postcard in hand, I declared my major. I majored in the classics.

As a classics major, I studied Greece and Rome, Latin and Greek—and I think it was through those studies that I developed a love for exploring other cultures and traveling.

Although Rome itself was fantastic, nothing will quite compare to the moment when I was walking on the outskirts of the city, looked up, and realized the structure overhead was not a bridge but the remains of an aqueduct. All my studies had come to life before me, and it was the first time I truly appreciated my education and the gift of travel—what it's like to marvel at another world that existed before me and will remain long after.

5 ΑΝΑΜΝΗΣΕΙΣ ΑΠΟ ΤΗΝ ΑΡΧΑΙΑ ΕΛΛΑΔΑ
Memoires de la Grece Ancienne
'Απόλλων καὶ Δάφνη
Apollon et Daphne
Apollon und Daphne
Apollon and Daphne

Greetings from...
the Place Chosen
by the Gods.
Christos

Linsey?
445 Conradi St.
Apt. 35
Tallahassee, FL 32304
U.S.A

32304/3464

Rome, Ital

drinks

GLOBAL

hot chocolate

SERVES 1

1 c nondairy milk

1 tbsp agave nectar

1 tbsp unsweetened cocoa

1 tsp vegan chocolate chips

ground cinnamon

Chef's Note If you have a Blendtec or Vitamix, you can place all ingredients in the blender and let it run for 3 minutes or until it's hot.

Like a lot of American kids, I grew up drinking Nestlé hot chocolate and was surprised to learn Nestlé is actually a Swiss company and hot chocolate is not an American invention. Hot chocolate dates back to the Mayans and Aztecs in Mesoamerica, but was popularized in Europe during the 16th and 17th centuries. You'll be hard pressed to find a drink with as much cultural diversity or history as hot chocolate; it is one of a few global comfort foods. This recipe reflects the American version of hot chocolate, which is thinner, but you can scale back on the liquid, or increase the chocolate, for a more European experience. By the way, the Mayans and Aztecs drank it unsweetened!

Combine nondairy milk, agave, cocoa, chocolate chips, and a dash or two cinnamon in a blender and whiz until smooth. Gently heat over low in a pan on the stove top or microwave using the beverage setting.

OTHER NAMES

Chocolat chaud **(French)**   Chocolademelk **(Dutch)**

Cioccolata densa **(Italian)**   Chocolate caliente **(Spanish)**

PER SERVING

(WITH DARK CHOCOLATE) Calories 128, Total Fat 4.4g, Carbohydrates 23.9g, Fiber 2.8g, Sugars 18.7g, Protein 2.3g

(WITH CHOCOLATE) Calories 135, Total Fat 4.8g, Carbohydrates 24.3g, Fiber 3g, Sugars 19.1g, Protein 2.4g

tinto de verano

PRONUNCIATION TIP
Tinto de verano sounds like "tin-toe day bear-an-no."
In Spanish, the letter "v" sounds more like a "b."

Tinto de verano, which translates to "red summer," is a popular drink in Spain during the summer months. It's similar to sangria but much simpler to prepare. I learned about it from Pablo, a local I befriended in Granada. When I told him I was there researching for my third cookbook, he insisted I include this beverage. His recipe was as follows: cheapest red wine you can find and Fanta.

SERVES 1

red wine (chilled)
orange soda (chilled)

There is no standard ratio between the red wine and orange soda; rather, the soda (Fanta, specifically) is on the table so everyone can add as much to their chilled red wine as they personally like. My personal preference is ¼ Fanta to ¾ wine, but increase the orange soda as you like.

PER SERVING
(¼ CUP FANTA TO ¾ CUP WINE)

Calories 177, Total Fat 0g,
Carbohydrates 12.4g, Fiber 0g,
Sugars 1.4g, Protein 0.1g

SPAIN

café con leche

PRONUNCIATION TIP
Leche sounds like "lay-chay."

SERVES 1

1 c nondairy milk
1 packet instant coffee
cinnamon (optional)

In Granada, Spain, I had some time to kill before my train arrived, so I dipped into a café near the station. Several travelers came in and out, ordering coffee. I always heard the waitress ask, "*¿Con leche?*" ("With milk?") but didn't think much of it until the man at the bar next to me ordered his coffee (with milk). I noticed the waitress had brought him a cup of warm milk with a packet of instant coffee—not coffee with a little side of milk or cream like it's served in the United States. I kept watching and noticed this was how it was always served any time someone wanted it "with milk." Finally, I asked the man next to me, "*¿Qué es eso? El nombre?*" ("What is that? The name?") and he replied, "*Café con leche*," which literally translates to "coffee with milk." I knew I had to try it at home with nondairy milk. And wow! It's really delicious!

Gently warm the nondairy milk (stove top is best). Once it's warmed, stir in coffee. You can also add a few shakes of cinnamon if desired.

PER SERVING | Calories 40, Total Fat 3g, Carbohydrates 2g, Fiber 1g, Sugars 0g, Protein 1g

sangria

My love for sangria knows no bounds. I drink it by the pitcher (yes, by myself!) when I'm in Spain. On my last trip to Barcelona, I watched a bartender make a pitcher of sangria, carefully jotting down everything he used. It's strong, but delicious and perfect for parties.

In a large pitcher, mix wine, vodka, orange juice, and seltzer, stirring to combine. Add cinnamon stick and sliced apples, if desired. Chill for several hours, then serve over ice.

SPAIN

SERVES 8

- 2 bottles cheap and fruity red wine
- 1 c orange-flavored vodka
- 1 orange (juice)
- 1 quart seltzer water
- 1 cinnamon stick (optional)
- 2 apples, sliced

Chef's Note Any orange-flavored liquor can be used in place of the vodka. I typically use Vodka Citron.

Chef's Note Any fizzy water can be used in place of seltzer. I've also seen people make (well, dilute) sangria with Sprite or 7-Up.

PER SERVING
(1 PITCHER)

Calories 243, Total Fat 0.1g, Carbohydrates 12.0g, Fiber 1.1g, Sugars 6.7g, Protein 0.3g

MEXICO

aqua fresca

Aqua frescas are popular fruit-flavored, nonalcoholic drinks in Mexico. The best way I can describe them is as water infused with the flavor of fruit, in contrast to a fruit juice or a smoothie. My favorite fruit to use is watermelon, but you can use mango, strawberries, peaches, papaya, cantaloupe, or any fruit that can be pureed into a silky smooth consistency. I also love it with cucumber, especially if you add fresh mint leaves to the pitcher.

MAKES 1 QUART

2 c chopped fruit
sweetener (optional)
1 lime (juice) (optional)
cheesecloth or sieve

Combine chopped fruit with 1 c water in your blender, pureeing until silky smooth, adding up to 1 c more water if necessary.

Wrap cheesecloth around the top of your blender container (or use a sieve) and strain the juice from the blender into a pitcher. I find the best method is to get it all in a cheesecloth and then squeeze it out using my hands.

Add 2 c water, or more if you prefer a more diluted drink, to the pitcher (to taste). You can also add sweetener, such as agave nectar or raw sugar if you wish, and lime juice, to taste (traditionally, ¼ c lime juice is added). Mix to combine and serve well chilled, over ice.

PER SERVING
(1 CUP, WITHOUT SWEETENER, VARIES WITH FRUIT USED)

Calories 23, Total Fat 0.1g, Carbohydrates 5.7g, Fiber 0g, Sugars 4.7g, Protein 0.5g

morir soñando

DOMINICAN REPUBLIC CARIBBEAN ISLANDS

PRONUNCIATION TIP
Morir soñando is pronounced "more-ear son-yahn-doh."

The name of this Dominican favorite means "to die dreaming," and it tastes like a Creamsicle in a glass!

Blend juice (fresh-squeezed is best), almond milk, ice, vanilla extract, and a pinch or two orange zest in a blender until smooth and creamy and no ice bits remain. Taste, adding agave nectar or other sweetener, if desired, and blend again if necessary. For a stronger orange flavor, add more juice. If the drink is too acidic or citrus-tasting, add more almond milk. (This is very much a "to taste" drink.)

SERVES 1

- 1 c fresh orange juice, with zest
- ¾ c almond milk
- 5–6 ice cubes
- ½ tsp vanilla extract
- 1 tbsp agave nectar (optional)

Chef's Note If you have a strong blender such as a Blendtec or Vitamix, you can peel two oranges and put them in whole.

PER SERVING
(WITHOUT SWEETENER)

Calories 150, Total Fat 2.8g, Carbohydrates 28.1g, Fiber 1.5g, Sugars 21.1g, Protein 2.5g

AFRICA

MOROCCO

moroccan mint tea

Morocco is just a boat ride away from Spain. You can actually see Spain and Gibraltar from Morocco and vice versa. Knowing Morocco was so close, I couldn't resist taking a day trip to Tangier. The city itself is full of culture and history—a little bit of Africa, Spain, and France is present. After spending several hours walking around marveling at the architecture and stunning tile mosaics, Scott and I dipped into a restaurant where we experienced Morocco's legendary hospitality. Although our meal was lovely (see Moroccan Vegetables, pg. 105), it was the mint tea they served us that really stole the show. In Morocco, tea is served at mealtimes, but it is also a drink of hospitality. Sweet and refreshing...you'll love this tea!

SERVES 1

- 1 green tea bag
- 1 full sprig of fresh mint (multiple leaves)
- ½–1 tsp agave nectar

Steep tea bag and mint in 1 c hot water for 4–5 minutes. Remove tea bag, but leave mint and add agave to taste. Cover your cup with a lid from a pot and steep for another 5 minutes. Remove mint leaves (if desired) and strain if necessary.

PER SERVING | Calories 11, Total Fat 0g, Carbohydrates 2.8g, Fiber 0g, Sugars 2.4g, Protein 0.1g

roasted barley tea

JAPAN

Roasted barley tea is a popular drink and coffee alternative in Japan, China, and Korea. I first had roasted barley tea at a macrobiotic restaurant in Los Angeles, and I have been making it at home ever since.

SERVES 3

¼ c pearl barley
agave nectar
(optional)

Add barley to a saucepan and turn heat to high to toast the barley. Give the pot a good shake every few minutes so the barley moves around and cooks evenly. Continue to toast barley until it turns deep brown and smells toasty. A few burned edges are okay, but don't totally burn all the barley. When the barley is brown and fragrant, slowly pour in 3 c water. It might bubble and fizzle—that's okay. Cover and bring to a boil. Once boiling, reduce to low and simmer for 15 minutes. Strain off tea (water) and enjoy hot or cold, adding agave or other sweetener to taste.

PER SERVING | Calories 0g, Total Fat 0g, Carbohydrates 0g, Fiber 0g, Sugars 0g, Protein 0g

BERMUDA

SERVES 1

½ c dark rum
½ c ginger beer
Angostura bitters
(optional)

Chef's Note You can find ginger beer at some health food stores and well-stocked supermarkets—it is usually kept in the tea and juice aisle. If you can't find ginger beer, ginger ale is an acceptable substitute.

dark 'n stormy

I was first introduced to this drink while living in St. Maarten and it is perhaps my absolute favorite drink of all time. In St. Maarten, a splash of Angostura bitters is sometimes added to the drink to enhance the flavors, but in Bermuda (where it originated) it's garnished with a slice of lime. I prefer to use Mount Gay or Myers's rum in this recipe.

Mix rum with ginger beer, add a dash of Angostura bitters (optional), and serve over ice. The drink should be a deep golden color. If it's too potent for you (some dark rums are rather strong), simply add more ginger beer.

PER SERVING | Calories 298, Total Fat 0g, Carbohydrates 10.7g, Sugars 10.6g, Protein 0.0g

radler

I'd met up with a Herbie in Hamburg and, at dinner, I ordered a beer (Hey! when in Rome . . . err, Germany!) and she ordered a radler. I'd never heard of a radler before, so she explained it to me—beer mixed with lemonade. I like beer and I like lemonade, but I couldn't possibly imagine the two together. It just sounded so awful . . . but curiosity eventually got the better of me, and I asked if I could have a sip. Shame on me. The radler was delicious and refreshing! Then, a few days later, I was at Oktoberfest and noticed that people often ordered Sprite (or a similar equivalent) and then poured it into their beer, making their own radler.

Combine equal parts beer and chilled Sprite or lemonade and serve.

GERMANY

SERVES 1

Beer (preferably German)

Sprite or lemonade

PER SERVING
(½ C BEER WITH ½ C LEMONADE)

Calories 101, Total Fat 0.1g, Carbohydrates 17.1g, Fiber 0g, Sugars 12.4g, Protein 0.0g

Seville, Spain (2011)

Seville, Spain (2006)

Seville, Spain, was one the cities I enjoyed most on my last trip through Europe, so I had planned to end my most recent trip there.

The covered streets in Seville are by far my favorite part, and it's amazing how well they actually cool the street down (Seville is HOT!).

And how crazy is this? I stumbled upon a random plaza where Scott and I had stopped for sangria on our trip five years earlier. (See the similarities in the picture above and on pg. 227.)

Seville, Spain (2011)

spices
& DIY

USA
ACADIA

CANADA

cajun seasoning

Commercial Cajun seasoning blends are often inconsistent when it comes to heat. Some brands are hotter than others, and the spices used in each can also vary. For these reasons, I prefer blending my own.

MAKES ½ CUP

2 tbsp sweet paprika

2 tbsp garlic powder (granulated)

1 tbsp cayenne pepper

1 tbsp chili powder

1 tbsp pepper

1 tbsp dried oregano or marjoram

1 tbsp onion powder (granulated)

½ tsp ground nutmeg or mace (optional)

Combine all spices and herbs thoroughly. Store in an airtight container.

Chef's Note If you want to substitute a commercial blend for convenience, I like McCormick's Cajun Seasoning from their Gourmet Collection and Badia's Louisiana Cajun seasoning.

PER SERVING (1 TBSP) | Calories 24, Total Fat 0.6g, Carbohydrates 4.9g, Fiber 1.9g, Sugars 0g, Protein 1.1g

shereé's cajun blend

MAKES ⅓ CUP

1 tsp white pepper

1 tsp garlic powder (granulated)

1 tsp onion powder (granulated)

1 tsp red pepper flakes, ground

1 tsp paprika

1 tsp black pepper

If you're looking for an alternative to my Cajun Seasoning, try my friend Shereé's blend. It's peppery!

Mix all ingredients together. Store in an airtight container.

PER SERVING (1 TSP) | Calories 360, Total Fat 6.0g, Carbohydrates 63.0g, Fiber 9.0g, Protein 12.0g

berberé

ETHIOPIA

Berberé, a spice blend, is a key ingredient in Ethiopian cooking. Although commercial blends exist, most of them are very hot and use cayenne pepper as the main ingredient. To keep control over the heat of the dish, I prefer blending a milder berberé myself. With this spice blend you can safely add 1 tsp to any recipe, but if you choose to substitute a premade blend for convenience, be cautious when adding it.

Whisk all spices together in nonstick skillet and toast over medium heat, stirring frequently to avoid burning. Once the spices are fragrant and smell toasty, turn off the heat and use a mortar and pestle to grind down into a fine powder. Store spice blend in an airtight container.

Chef's Note Although not the same, in a pinch you can substitute cayenne powder for berberé.

MAKES ¾ CUP

- 2 tbsp cayenne powder, or to taste
- 4 tbsp sweet paprika
- 1 tsp ground fenugreek
- ¾ tsp ground cardamom
- ½ tsp ground coriander
- ½ tsp ground cumin
- ½ tsp ground nutmeg or mace
- ½ tsp ground ginger
- ¼ tsp ground cinnamon
- ¼ tsp ground allspice
- ¼ tsp turmeric
- ⅛ tsp ground cloves

PER SERVING (1 TBSP) | Calories 10, Total Fat 0.4g, Carbohydrates 1.8g, Fiber 1.1g, Sugars 0g, Protein 0.5g

Chef's Note If you like spicy and hot food, feel free to add more cayenne powder to this blend or simply add more cayenne powder or hot sauce to the dish.

GLOBAL

poultry seasoning mix

MAKES ¼ CUP

- 1 tbsp dried rosemary
- 1 tbsp dried thyme
- 1 tbsp rubbed sage (not powdered)
- 1 tbsp dried marjoram or oregano
- 1 tbsp dried parsley or basil

Chef's Note If you can find granulated (not powdered) poultry seasoning that isn't a rub, feel free to use it for convenience rather than blending your own. I like Cost Plus, World Market's generic brand.

This savory herb mixture is my favorite seasoning. You can substitute store-bought poultry blends for convenience; just be sure they are not powdered. The consistency should be like dried basil. In a pinch, Italian seasoning may be substituted.

Grind herbs together in a mortar and pestle until coarse like the consistency of sea salt, but not powdered. Store in an airtight container.

PER SERVING
(1 TBSP)

Calories 10, Total Fat 0.4g, Carbohydrates 2.0g, Fiber 1.3g, Sugars 0g, Protein 0.3g

date syrup

Date syrup is Iraq's maple syrup.

IRAQ

Blend dates with 1 c warm water. If it seems watery, add dates. Note that it will thicken as it cools. If it becomes too thick, thin it with water or juice. Add vanilla or maple extract, if desired.

MAKES 1 CUP

1 c dates
vanilla extract (optional)
maple extract (optional)

PER SERVING
(1 TBSP)

Calories 42, Total Fat 0.1g, Carbohydrates 11.9g, Fiber 1.2g, Sugars 9.4g, Protein 0.4g

vegan mayo

Here is my easy and inexpensive recipe for making your own low-fat vegan mayo at home.

SPAIN

Blend tofu with Dijon and vinegar until creamy. Add a few drops of lemon juice and agave nectar and blend again. Taste and add more lemon, agave nectar, or Dijon as needed. Serve chilled.

Chef's Note In a pinch or for soy-free, substitute plain vegan yogurt for vegan mayo.

MAKES 1 CUP

1 12.3-oz pkg Mori-Nu tofu
2–3 tbsp Dijon mustard
2 tsp distilled white vinegar
lemon juice
agave nectar

PER SERVING
(1 TBSP)

Calories 10, Total Fat 0.2g, Carbohydrates 0.3g, Fiber 0g, Sugars 0g, Protein 1.6g

GLOBAL

no-beef broth

There are a few commercial mock beef broth bouillon cubes on the market, but I find all of them a little too salty for my taste. This is my DIY version.

MAKES 1 CUP

- 1 tbsp soy sauce
- 1 tbsp nutritional yeast
- ½ tsp Vegan Worcestershire Sauce (pg. 237)
- ¼ tsp onion powder (granulated)
- ¼ tsp garlic powder (granulated)
- ¼ tsp ground ginger

In a medium saucepan, whisk all ingredients together with 1 c water until well combined. Bring to a boil and simmer for 1 minute. If you used low-sodium soy sauce, you might want to add a little salt.

PER SERVING (1 CUP)	Calories 27, Total Fat 0.2g, Carbohydrates 4.3g, Fiber 1.1g, Sugars 0.7g, Protein 2.7g

Chef's Note If you use this broth in a soup recipe, add a bay leaf during cooking.

oat flour

Although you can purchase oat flour commercially, it's easy and inexpensive to make at home.

MAKES 1 CUP

- 1 c instant oats
- - or -
- 1 c plus 2 tbsp rolled oats

Place oats in a blender (make sure the container is completely dry) and whiz until it is a smooth, very fine flour.

PER SERVING (1 CUP)	Calories 360, Total Fat 6.0g, Carbohydrates 63.0g, Fiber 9.0g, Sugars 0g, Protein 12.0g

mushroom broth

FRANCE

This recipe was passed on to me by the head chef of Millennium in San Francisco, and it's a great way to use up mushroom stems.

MAKES ABOUT 4 CUPS

mushroom stems
¼–½ onion
soy sauce (optional)

Bring 4 c water to a boil. Add mushroom stems and onion. Cover and bring to a boil again, then simmer for about 1 hour, until water becomes cloudy and beige and onion is practically falling apart. Place your colander or strainer over a bowl, so you can pour the liquid into the bowl while the colander catches the mushrooms and onions. Use a spatula or small bowl to press the excess liquid out of the mushrooms and onions, then discard. Add soy sauce to the resulting broth if desired (I like to do this to salt my broth slightly and give it a richer color). Use within 2 days or freeze.

PER CUP | Calories 7, Total Fat 0.1g, Carbohydrates 1.2g, Fiber 0g, Sugars 0.6g, Protein 0.6g

GLOBAL

no-chicken broth powder

Frontier makes a decent vegetarian chicken-flavored broth powder, though it contains corn syrup. There are a few commercial mock chicken broth bouillon cubes on the market as well, but I find them a little too salty for my taste. This is my DIY version.

MAKES APPROXIMATELY 25 SERVINGS

- 1⅓ c nutritional yeast
- 2 tbsp onion powder (granulated)
- 1 tbsp garlic powder (granulated)
- 1 tsp dried thyme
- 1 tsp rubbed sage (not powdered)
- 1 tsp paprika
- ½ tsp turmeric
- ¼ tsp celery seed
- ¼ tsp dried parsley

Combine all ingredients and grind with a mortar and pestle into a fine powder. Store in an airtight container, such as a clear glass jar.

PER SERVING (1 TBSP) | Calories 12, Total Fat 0.1g, Carbohydrates 1.7g, Fiber 0.7g, Sugars 0g, Protein 1.3g

Chef's Note No-Chicken Broth: Mix 1 tablespoon of the mixture with 1 c warm water to yield 1 c broth.

vegan worcestershire sauce

ENGLAND

Most commercial Worcestershire sauces contain anchovies, although there are a few vegetarian brands on the market. While nothing beats the ease of bottled sauce, this DIY recipe is allergen-free and very inexpensive to make. Worcestershire sauce is traditionally used as a condiment for meat, and consequently is a great marinade for veggie burgers and acts as a flavoring agent in many meat substitute recipes.

Whisk vinegar through cinnamon together and add a light dash of cayenne (or chili powder) and a light dash of allspice (or cloves) with ¼ cup water until well combined. Add salt if desired. Store in an airtight container in the fridge.

Chef's Note Yeast extract, such as Marmite and Vegemite, can be used in place of Worcestershire sauce if Worcestershire sauce is being used as an ingredient in something and not as a condiment or marinade.

MAKES 1 CUP

- 6 tbsp apple cider vinegar
- 2 tbsp tamari
- 1 tbsp brown sugar, or 1 tsp molasses
- 2 tsp prepared mustard (any)
- ¼ tsp onion powder (granulated)
- ¼ tsp garlic powder (granulated)
- ¼ tsp ground ginger
- ⅛ tsp ground cinnamon
- cayenne pepper or chili powder
- allspice or ground cloves

Chef's Note Low-sodium soy sauce may be substituted for the tamari.

PER SERVING (1 TSP) | Calories 6, Total Fat 0g, Carbohydrates 0.9g, Fiber 0g, Sugars 0.6g, Protein 0.3g

GLOBAL

vegetable broth

MAKES 4 CUPS

- 1 onion (any), peeled
- 1 large carrot
- 1 celery stalk
- 3–4 garlic cloves, peeled
- 3–5 oz fresh or dried herbs (any)
- 1–2 tsp yellow miso
- 4 whole black peppercorns
- 1 bay leaf

PLUS ANY THREE OF THE FOLLOWING

- 1 small brown potato
- 2–4 small red potatoes
- 1 c mushrooms
- 1 bell pepper, seeded
- 1 medium turnip
- 1 medium zucchini
- 1 parsnip
- 1 leek

Nothing beats the ease of premade broth or bouillon cubes, but homemade vegetable broth is superior in comparison. It's also a great way to use up veggies that are on their way to expiration. I like to use sweet onions, potatoes, parsnips, turnips, and fresh fennel.

Transfer onion, carrot, celery, garlic, and your three additional veggie selections to a large pot. If using dried herbs, grab each green one you have on hand and give it a good shake into the pot. Otherwise, add fresh dill or any complementary fresh herbs you have. Add 1–2 tsp miso, peppercorns, and bay leaf. Add 8 c cold water, or 10 c if your vegetable selections are particularly big. Cover and bring to a boil. Reduce heat to low and simmer until the vegetables are falling apart, about 1 hour. Turn off heat and allow to cool to warm. Use tongs or a spoon to remove bay leaf and vegetables. Grab a cheesecloth or fine strainer and strain liquid into a plastic container. Cool to room temperature, then store in the fridge for up to 3 days. After 3 days, store in freezer in 1-c measurements.

Chef's Note You can omit the miso and add salt to taste for a soy-free vegetable broth.

PER SERVING (1 CUP) | Calories 49, Total Fat 0.4g, Carbohydrates 10.6g, Fiber 2.2g, Sugars 4.1g, Protein 2.2g

sour cream

This sour cream is quick and easy to make, with a fraction of the fat of dairy and commercial vegan sour creams.

ISRAEL

Combine tofu with 2 tbsp lemon juice, vinegar, salt, mustard powder, a few drops of agave nectar, and a light dash of garlic powder and blend until smooth and creamy. Taste and add more lemon and/or sweetener if necessary or desired. Stir in dill (if using) before serving.

MAKES 1 CUP

- 1 12.3-oz pkg Mori-Nu firm tofu
- 2–4 tbsp lemon juice
- ½ tsp distilled white vinegar
- ⅛ tsp salt
- 1 tsp dry mustard powder
- agave nectar
- garlic powder (granulated)
- 1 tsp dried or fresh dill (optional)

 **PER SERVING** (1 TBSP, WITH 1 TBSP AGAVE NECTAR) | Calories 13, Total Fat 0.2g, Carbohydrates 1.4g, Fiber 0g, Sugars 1.1g, Protein 1.6g

Chef's Note This sour cream should last at least a week. It depends on your fridge, container, and how fresh the tofu was when you bought it. When tofu goes bad, you know it! It'll turn pink and smell foul.

I was at the tail end of my trip in Paris, France, when Steve Jobs died. I was catching up on e-mail in the lobby when I glanced up at the TV in the bar to see what everyone was staring at so intently.

I could feel the tears welling up in my eyes immediately. Steve Jobs was someone I admired, and his words had often been a comfort to me.

When I started Happy Herbivore, friends and colleagues had little belief that my blog would obtain readership because I did not use oil and tried to make everything healthy—by using whole-wheat flour instead of all-purpose, for example.

They were even more dubious when I announced I was leaving the law to pursue Happy Herbivore as a career. I had my own doubts and fears too, and the way I overcame them was by reminding myself of Steve Jobs's famous quote, *"Don't let the noise of others' opinions drown out your own inner voice ... Have the courage to follow your heart and intuition. They somehow already know what you truly want to become."*

In that moment in Paris, I realized I had finally become the person I was supposed to be. I was finally living the life I had always dreamed of and I had finally, finally come to accept that when you do something for other people rather than yourself, you will not find happiness.

I had found happiness. I had found my way home. And most importantly, I had found myself.

usa

USA

bacon bits

Bacon Bits and other similar brands at the grocery store are usually accidentally vegan. However, they often have corn syrup, hydrogenated oils, food colorings, and weird preservatives that aren't so healthy. Here is a quick and easy recipe to make them at home.

MAKES 1 CUP

2 tbsp soy sauce

1½ tsp liquid smoke

2 tsp pure maple syrup

¼ tsp garlic powder (granulated)

⅛ tsp paprika

½ c TVP or TSP

Combine soy sauce, liquid smoke, 1 tbsp water, maple syrup, garlic powder, and paprika in a small saucepan and bring to a boil. Once it's boiling, immediately turn off the heat and stir in TVP or TSP. Continue to stir until all the liquid has been absorbed. Add salt as needed. Next, you'll need to crisp up and dehydrate the bits. You can either set your toaster oven to 200°F and toast the crumbs, shaking the tray every 2 minutes to prevent burning and repeating until crisp, or fry in a nonstick pan until crispy, stirring often.

PER SERVING | Calories 27, Total Fat 0g, Carbohydrates 3.3g, Fiber 1.1g, Sugars 1.8g, Protein 3.3g

USA

blueberry cornbread muffins

Combining two of my favorite American comfort foods: cornbread and blueberry muffins!

Chef's Note Did you know that muffins as we know them are fairly unique to the United States? The American English term muffin refers to what others regions call quick breads, only muffins are also baked in small portions.

Preheat oven to 350°F. Grease muffin tin and set aside or use silicone cups. In a mixing bowl, whisk together flour, cornmeal, baking powder, baking soda, salt, and lemon zest until well combined. Mix in syrup, sugar, and applesauce, stirring a few times to incorporate. Add nondairy milk and stir a few more times. Then mix in blueberries until batter is just combined. Spoon into muffin tins and bake 15–18 minutes, or until a toothpick inserted comes out clean.

MAKES 12

- 1½ c white whole-wheat flour
- ½ c fine yellow cornmeal
- 2 tsp baking powder
- 1 tsp baking soda
- salt (optional)
- 1–2 tsp lemon zest
- ¼ c pure maple syrup
- ¼ c raw sugar
- 1 c unsweetened applesauce
- ½ c nondairy milk
- ¾ c wild blueberries

Chef's Note You can find wild blueberries in the freezer section of most grocery stores. They're much smaller than regular blueberries.

PER MUFFIN | Calories 120, Total Fat 0.6g, Carbohydrates 27.7g, Fiber 2.5g, Sugars 11.5g, Protein 2.6g

HAWAII

sunshine muffins

MAKES 12

- 2 c white whole-wheat flour
- 1 tsp baking soda
- ½ tsp baking powder
- 1 20-oz can crushed pineapple, undrained
- 1–2 tsp lemon zest
- 1 tsp vanilla extract
- ½–1 c raw sugar

Chef's Note I find these muffins get sweeter and more flavorful as they cool.

After my first year of law school, I spent a portion of my summer in Maui, staying with a friend and her Hawaiian family. I fell deeply in love with fresh pineapple and mango while visiting and rediscovered the delicate taste of both tropical fruits while living in St. Maarten. These muffins celebrate pineapple's delicate yet complex, sweet flavor. I make them anytime I need to be transported back to paradise, if only in my mind.

Preheat oven to 350°F. Grease a muffin tin or use silicone cups and set aside. In a medium bowl, whisk all dry ingredients together until well combined. Add pineapple, lemon zest, vanilla, sugar, and a pinch of salt if desired, stirring until just combined. Gently spoon batter into muffin cups and bake 15–20 minutes, or until a toothpick inserted in the center comes out clean.

PER MUFFIN

Calories 125, Total Fat 0.3g, Carbohydrates 28.8g, Fiber 2g, Sugars 13.8g, Protein 2.8g

EXTRA SUGAR Calories 158, Total Fat 0.3g, Carbohydrates 37.1g, Fiber 2g, Sugars 22.1g, Protein 2.8g

bran muffins

USA

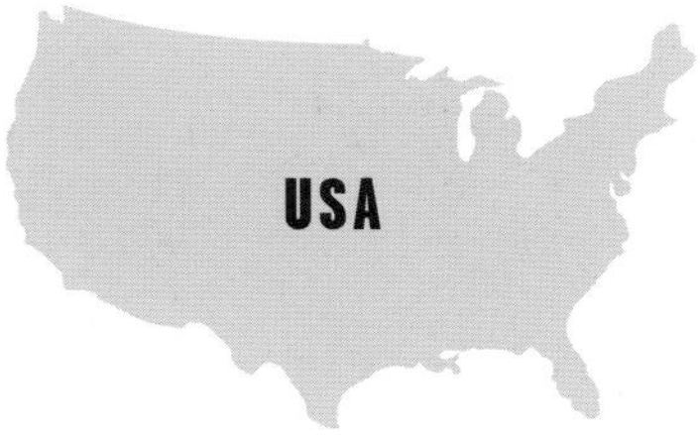

My sister, Courtney, showed up at my house one day with a bag of bran, saying, "As your sister, I only have one request. Please make me bran muffins." Her request was specific: It had to be a plain bran muffin with no nuts or dried fruit (though you can add them if you like). I made several different batches, and these were her favorite. Bonus: I really like them too!

Preheat oven to 350°F. Grease muffin tin and set aside or use silicone cups. In a mixing bowl, whisk bran with flour, baking powder, and baking soda. Add remaining ingredients, stirring to combine. If batter appears too dry, add another 1–2 tbsp nondairy milk. Bran batter is a bit thicker than most muffin batters, but it shouldn't be dry or floury. Spoon batter into muffin cups and bake 15 minutes, or until firm to the touch and a toothpick inserted in the center comes out clean.

MAKES 6

- ¾ c bran
- ½ c white whole-wheat flour
- ½ tsp baking powder
- ½ tsp baking soda
- 6 tbsp nondairy milk
- ¼ c pure maple syrup
- 3 tbsp unsweetened applesauce
- ¼ tsp vanilla extract

PER MUFFIN | Calories 103, Total Fat 1.1g, Carbohydrates 20.6g, Fiber 6.2g, Sugars 8.9g, Protein 3.4g

USA

stuffed acorn squash

SERVES 2

1 acorn squash
½ c quinoa
1¼ c vegetable broth
¼ tsp mild curry powder
cinnamon
¼ c raisins
1 c spinach, finely chopped

Stuffed squash is a classic Thanksgiving dish. This is one of my favorite dishes to serve at dinner parties or during the holidays. It's so easy to make and yet it presents beautifully—it's simply exquisite and the kind of dish that will wow anyone.

Preheat oven to 400°F. Cut acorn squash in half, place cut side down on a cookie sheet, and bake 30–35 minutes, until fork-tender. Meanwhile, combine quinoa, vegetable broth, curry powder, a few dashes of cinnamon (about ⅛ tsp), and raisins in a pot. Bring to a boil, immediately reduce to low, and cook for 15 minutes, or until liquid evaporates. If quinoa is not fluffy after 15 minutes, add more vegetable broth and cook longer. (Sometimes the raisins will absorb the liquid also, so more is needed to cook the quinoa. I find this is particularly true with electric stoves.) After quinoa is done, stir in spinach, add another dash or two of cinnamon, plus salt if desired, then cover and set aside, away from heat.

Once acorn squash is done, flip it over and scoop out seedy matter. Then use a sharp knife to cut the point off each base so the acorn bowls sit upright and don't fall over. Spoon quinoa mixture into squash and serve warm.

PER SERVING | Calories 302, Total Fat 2.8g, Carbohydrates 65.8g, Fiber 7.2g, Sugars 11.4g, Protein 8.4g

lentil loaf

USA

Nothing says American like Mom's meatloaf! This Lentil Loaf hits the spot any time I'm in the mood for a comforting down-home-cooking kind of meal. Serve with steamed mixed vegetables and mashed potatoes, such as Roasted Garlic Mashed Potatoes (p. 260).

Combine lentils with vegetable broth in a pot, cover, and bring to a boil. Once boiling, reduce to low and simmer for 20 minutes or until lentils are cooked (soft, but not mushy) and the liquid has evaporated. Meanwhile, place onion, carrot, and celery in a food processor or blender and pulse until they are finely chopped—the smaller the better, but don't pulverize. Transfer to a large mixing bowl and mix with ketchup, mustard, soy sauce, nutritional yeast, and Italian seasoning and set aside. Preheat oven to 350°F and grease a standard bread pan or line with parchment paper, allowing the paper to rise 2 inches above the top of the pan. Once lentils are cooked, transfer to blender or food processor and pulse a few times so most of the lentils are chewed up, but some half lentils remain and it's not total mush. Transfer chopped lentils to the mixing bowl, add oats, and stir to combine. Pour mixture into bread pan, pressing it into every corner and packing it down firmly with a spatula. Bake 40–50 minutes uncovered, or until firm with a crisp outer coating. Let cool in the pan 10 minutes before serving. Place a plate on top of the pan and flip over, so the loaf flips onto the plate.

SERVES 8

- 1 c dried lentils
- 2 c vegetable broth
- 1 small onion
- 1 carrot, skinned
- 2 celery stalks
- ¼ c ketchup
- 2 tbsp yellow mustard
- 2 tbsp low-sodium soy sauce
- 2 tbsp nutritional yeast
- 1 tbsp Italian seasoning
- 1 c instant oats

Chef's Note If you have rolled oats, you can pulse them a few times in your blender or food processor to make them smaller—do this first while the container is still dry.

PER SLICE

Calories 143, Total Fat 1.6g, Carbohydrates 24.3g, Fiber 9.1g, Sugars 3.6g, Protein 8.8g

USA

cajun stuffed mushrooms

These mushrooms will dazzle anyone they're served to. They're ridiculously easy to make and sure to please—my go-to party appetizer!

MAKES 12 MUSHROOMS

- ¼ c vegetable broth
- ¼ c red bell pepper, finely diced
- ¼ c celery, finely diced
- ¼ c onion, finely diced
- 4 garlic cloves, minced
- 1 tsp Cajun Seasoning (pg. 230)
- 1 c spinach, finely diced
- hot sauce (optional)
- 14 oz white mushrooms

Chef's Note You can make these mushrooms ahead: stuff mushrooms, then store in the fridge and bake later.

Chef's Note You can use the mushroom stems you removed to make Mushroom Broth (p. 235).

Chef's Note These mushrooms were inspired by a Weight Watchers recipe my colleagues used to bring to Christmas parties.

Preheat oven to 350°F. Line a large skillet with a thin layer of broth. Add bell pepper, celery, onion, and garlic, and sauté over high heat until bell peppers are soft and onions are translucent, about 2–3 minutes. Stir in Cajun Seasoning, adding hot sauce to taste if desired. Add spinach and a splash of broth if necessary to prevent sticking, and stir. Continue stirring until spinach is darker green and soft, about a minute or less. Turn off heat and set aside. Remove stems from mushrooms and place mushrooms bottoms up in a lightly greased or nonstick muffin tin or on a silicone mat. Stuff each mushroom with the spinach filling and bake 10–15 minutes, until mushrooms are tender but not so cooked that they are mushy or falling apart. Serve warm.

PER MUSHROOM Calories 12, Total Fat 0.1g, Carbohydrates 2g, Fiber 0.5g, Sugars 0.8g, Protein 1.2g

USA

roasted garlic mashed potatoes

Mashed potatoes are a comfort food for me. Here, cauliflower is a surprise ingredient. Along with the roasted garlic, it adds a ton of flavor while also making mashed potatoes a little less starchy.

Preheat oven to 375°F. Grease a cookie sheet or line with parchment paper and set aside. Microwave, boil, or steam potato, then dice. Meanwhile, place cauliflower stem side down on a cutting board and cut end pieces into florets, discarding the stem. Place florets on cookie sheet and sprinkle with salt and pepper, if desired, then bake for 10 minutes. After 10 minutes, flip cauliflower over and sprinkle with half of the minced garlic. Bake another 5 minutes, then add remaining garlic and cook until garlic is fragrant and cauliflower is fork-tender and lightly golden, about another 5 minutes (20–25 total).

Transfer cauliflower and garlic to a food processor and add cubed cooked potato, plus nondairy milk, nutritional yeast, and Dijon. Allow motor to run for about a minute. Stop, scrape sides, and let it run for another 10–20 seconds, adding broth as necessary to achieve a mashed potato consistency.

Serve warm sprinkled with smoked paprika.

USA

peppered mushroom gravy

MAKES 1 CUP

- 2–3 green onions
- 1 c vegetable broth
- 2 garlic cloves, minced
- 2 c white mushrooms, sliced
- 1 c nondairy milk
- 1½ tsp Dijon mustard
- 1 tbsp nutritional yeast
- 2 tbsp chickpea flour

PER SERVING
(¼ CUP)

Calories 60, Total Fat 1.5g, Carbohydrates 9g, Fiber 2.7g, Sugars 1.8g, Protein 4.1g

This Southern-inspired gravy is crazy universal and crazy—crazy good! Serve it on greens, grains, chickpeas, or mashed potatoes or thin it out a little with extra non-dairy milk to create a creamy pasta sauce.

Mince white and light green parts of green onions and set aside temporarily. Slice dark green parts into 2-inch pieces, then slice in half longways and set aside. Line a skillet with a thin layer of broth. Add garlic and minced onion and sauté over high heat until the garlic starts to turn golden and most of the liquid has cooked off. Add remaining broth, bring to a boil, and add mushrooms. Once boiling, reduce to low and add leftover green onion pieces. Continue to sauté, stirring regularly, until mushrooms get soft and release their juices. Meanwhile, whisk nondairy milk with Dijon, nutritional yeast and chickpea flour until well combined. Pour into skillet when mushrooms are ready and stir to combine. Crank heat to high and bring to a near boil, then reduce to low immediately. Continue to cook and stir until it thickens into a gravy. Add black pepper and salt to taste (I like it rather peppery).

golden scallion gravy

USA

This gravy whips up quickly and is quite lovely with its rich golden coloring and little slices of green onion, making it perfect for family and holiday gatherings. It also goes with just about anything, but it really shines over mashed potatoes and green beans.

Whisk all ingredients together and bring to a near boil. Once almost boiling, reduce to low and simmer, stirring constantly for a minute or two, until the mixture thickens into a gravy. Add salt and pepper to taste and more Dijon mustard, if desired. I am pretty generous with both salt and pepper, especially the black pepper, in this recipe.

MAKES 1 CUP

- ½ c vegetable broth
- ½ c nondairy milk
- 2 green onions, sliced
- 1 tbsp nutritional yeast
- ½ tsp onion powder (granulated)
- ½ tsp garlic powder (granulated)
- ¼–½ tsp Dijon mustard
- 1 tbsp white whole-wheat flour

Chef's Note Any gluten-free flour (such as brown rice flour or chickpea flour) can be substituted to make this recipe gluten-free.

PER SERVING
(ABOUT ¼ CUP)

Calories 27, Total Fat 0.6g, Carbohydrates 4.3g, Fiber 1.2g, Sugars 0.6g, Protein 1.8g

carolina casserole

USA

This hearty casserole is a take on the Southern New Year's classic, Hoppin' John—a great way to start the new year!

Preheat oven to 400°F. Grease a square baking pan or line with parchment paper. Drain tomato juices into a skillet, then chop tomatoes into smaller pieces and set aside. Add water so a thin layer of liquid covers the skillet. Sauté onion, celery, and garlic over high heat until onions are translucent and water has evaporated, about 3–4 minutes. Mix in 2–3 tsp Cajun Seasoning, tomatoes, and ¼ c broth. Add greens and more broth if necessary to prevent sticking. Continue to sauté until the greens are lightly cooked and still brightly colored. Add beans and remaining broth and set aside.

In a small mixing bowl, whisk cornmeal, baking powder, and a pinch of salt, if desired. You can also add 1–2 tbsp sugar for a sweet cornbread topping. Stir in nondairy milk and applesauce. It should be thick, but spreadable and not dry. Pour bean–collard mixture into your baking dish and pat down firmly with a spatula. Spread cornbread mixture evenly on top and bake 30–35 minutes, or until the cornbread is a deep golden brown, cracked, and firm to the touch. Let casserole sit away from heat for 15 minutes before serving.

SERVES 6

- 1 15-oz can diced tomatoes, undrained
- 1 small onion, diced small
- 1 celery, minced
- 4 garlic cloves, minced
- 2–3 tsp Cajun Seasoning (pg. 230)
- 2–3 c collard greens, chopped
- ½ c vegetable broth, divided
- 1 15-oz can black eyed peas, drained and rinsed

TOPPING

- 1 c fine cornmeal
- 1½ tsp baking powder
- 1–2 tbsp raw sugar (optional)
- ¾ c nondairy milk
- ¼ c unsweetened applesauce

PER SERVING | Calories 166, Total Fat 2g, Carbohydrates 32.6g, Fiber 5.9g, Sugars 3.7g, Protein 7g

USA

MAKES 2 CUPS

TO REPLACE 2 CUPS OF FLOUR

1 c brown rice flour
½ c tapioca starch
½ c potato starch
plus 1 tsp xanthan gum (or guar gum) for every 2 c this blend

brody's gluten-free flour blend

Brody's Bakery (brodysbakery.com) is Kansas City's only all-vegan and gluten-free bakery. This is their tried and true recipe for gluten-free all-purpose flour and it's used in all of their scrumptious goodies. "We've burned through a lot of gluten-free flour blends and this seems to be the only one that (a) no one can tell is gluten-free and (b) works with any recipe, be it cooking or baking," says Katie Olson, owner and baker.

Mix all ingredients together. Store in an airtight container and use cup for cup any time whole-wheat or all-purpose flour is called for in a recipe.

PER SERVING
(¼ C)

Calories 46, Total Fat 0.6g, Carbohydrates 33.5g, Fiber 1g, Sugars 0g, Protein 1.4g

*COMPARE TO WHOLE WHEAT
Calories 114, Total Fat 0.3g, Carbohydrates 23.9g, Fiber 0.8g, Sugars 0g, Protein 3.2g

winter confetti salad

USA

This refreshing salad is seasonal during the winter months when most produce is out of season. It also presents beautifully, making it a perfect addition to your holiday menu.

In a mixing bowl, combine parsnip, apple, celery, rice, and radishes. Next, add mayo, Dijon, orange juice, and orange zest, stirring to combine. Stir in half of the green onions and use the remaining onions for garnish. Serve chilled.

PER SERVING | Calories 76, Total Fat 0.5g, Carbohydrates 16.7g, Fiber 2.8g, Sugars 5.1g, Protein 2.0g

SERVES 4

- ½ parsnip, skinned and finely diced
- ¼ red apple, sliced thinly
- 1 celery stalk, finely chopped
- ¾–1 c cooked rice
- 1 c radishes, thinly sliced
- 1 tbsp Vegan Mayo (p. 233)
- 1 tsp Dijon mustard
- ½ orange (juice and zest)
- 2 green onions, sliced

Chef's Note If you double this recipe, you may want to be careful with the amount of Dijon you use.

USA

creamy mushroom barley

MAKES 5 CAKES

- 8 oz brown mushrooms
- 1 c barley
- 1½ c vegetable broth
- 1½ tsp thyme, divided
- 2 garlic cloves, minced
  smoked paprika
- 6 tbsp nondairy milk
- 1 tbsp low-sodium soy sauce
- 1 tbsp nutritional yeast
- 1 tsp Dijon mustard
- ½ tsp onion powder (granulated)
- ½ tsp garlic powder (granulated)
- 2–3 c spinach, chopped

Chef's Note I like to scoop the barley using a ½-c measuring cup, packed tightly, to form "cakes" on my plate (makes 5).

Barley is probably the most underutilized grain in my kitchen, so I set out to create a recipe that not only uses barley but celebrates it.

Check barley package to determine water-to-barley ratio (1½–3 c water is usually called for). Remove stems from mushrooms and save for another use (e.g., Mushroom Broth [pg. 235]). Slice thinly. Combine in a medium pot with barley, water or broth, 1 tsp thyme, garlic, and a few light dashes of smoked paprika. Cover and bring to a boil. Once boiling, reduce to low and simmer until barley is soft and liquid is evaporated, about 45 minutes. If barley is not completely cooked, add more liquid and continue to cook until barley is soft. Once barley is done, add nondairy milk, soy sauce, nutritional yeast, Dijon mustard, onion powder, garlic powder, remaining thyme, and a few more dashes of smoked paprika, stirring to combine. If you want it a little wetter with a "gravy," add a splash more nondairy milk. Add salt and pepper to taste, then stir in spinach (while it's still piping hot). Stir constantly until spinach cooks slightly and folds into the barley, about 45 seconds.

PER SERVING | Calories 162, Total Fat 1.4g, Carbohydrates 31.8g, Fiber 7.7g, Sugars 1.4g, Protein 7.5g

USA

skillet green bean casserole

SERVES 2

- 1 c vegetable broth
- 1 onion, diced
- 2 garlic cloves, minced
- 1 c mushrooms, thinly sliced
- ½ lb green beans, trimmed
- 1 tbsp poultry seasoning (granulated not powdered)
- 1 tbsp Dijon mustard
- ½ tsp thyme
- ½ tsp sage
- nutmeg
- ½ c nondairy milk
- 2 tbsp nutritional yeast
- 1 tbsp cornstarch
- toasted bread crumbs (optional)
- fried onions (optional)

I love this American favorite and it makes for a quick and easy meal.

Line a skillet with a thin layer of broth and sauté the onions and garlic over high heat until onions are translucent, about a minute. Reduce heat to medium and add the remaining broth plus mushrooms, green beans, poultry seasoning, Dijon mustard, thyme, sage, and a dash of nutmeg, stirring to coat the mushrooms with seasonings. Continue to cook until the mushrooms are soft and the green beans are cooked but still crisp, about 7 minutes. Meanwhile, in a measuring glass or small bowl, whisk nondairy milk with nutritional yeast and cornstarch. Once green beans and mushrooms are cooked, pour in the nondairy milk mixture. Stir a few times and allow the mixture to thicken. Once it thickens slightly, turn off heat. Add salt and pepper to taste, then spoon the casserole mixture into bowls and top with toasted bread crumbs or fried onions if desired.

Chef's Note In a pinch, you can use Italian seasoning instead of poultry seasoning.

PER SERVING Calories 145, Total Fat 2.0g, Carbohydrates 26.9g, Fiber 8.5g, Sugars 5.1g, Protein 9.2g

red wine substitute

USA

This recipe is courtesy of my friend Shereé, who doesn't drink wine. She uses it in any recipe calling for red wine. She says, "This recipe was born by seeking for that rich, deep flavor one gets with the use of red wine in many recipes, for an alcohol-free home. I needed to find a way to still have that robust flavor that red wine can bring to a dish. Trial and error brought to life this recipe, and the family loves it. It can be used in stews and doubled with ease for larger recipes."

MAKES ½ CUP

- 2 tbsp Vegan Worcestershire Sauce (pg. 237)
- 2 tbsp red wine vinegar
- 2 tbsp tomato paste
- ½ tsp Better Than Bouillon No Beef Base

Put all the ingredients plus ½ c water into a saucepan, cover, and bring to a boil. Once boiling, reduce to low and simmer, cooking until it reduces by about half. Pour mixture into a measuring cup, adding extra broth if necessary to reach ½ c. Replaces wine in a 1:1 ratio.

PER SERVING (½ CUP) | Calories 68, Total Fat 0.1g, Carbohydrates 13.3g, Fiber 1.3g, Sugars 10.0g, Protein 1.9g

USA

refried white beans

SERVES 2

- 3 green onions
- ½ c vegetable broth
- 4 garlic cloves, minced
- 1 carrot, skinned and finely chopped
- 1 tsp ground cumin
- 1 tsp tomato paste
- ¼ c diced green chilies
- 1 15-oz can white beans (any kind), undrained
- hot sauce
- cayenne pepper (optional)

Chef's Note Any white beans will do here—cannellini, butter bean, or navy.

Chef's Note Ketchup may be substituted for the tomato paste.

A friend of mine who is originally from Texas told me about a popular Tex-Mex potluck favorite—*frijoles blancos refritos*, refried beans made with white beans rather than the traditional pinto bean. These beans are so easy to make and really delicious. Sorry, pintos!

Slice dark green parts off of the green onions and set aside. Chop off rooty bottoms and discard, then mince white and light green parts. Line a skillet with a thin layer of vegetable broth and sauté minced onion and garlic until most of the water has cooked off, about 2 minutes. Add carrots, cumin, tomato paste, and green chilies, plus enough broth to line the skillet with a thin layer of liquid. Sauté until carrot pieces are tender and most of the liquid has evaporated, about 2 minutes. Add beans with their liquid, and stir to combine. Reduce heat to low and mash beans well with a fork or potato masher a few times. You still want some whole and half beans, not a refried consistency. It will look very soupy; don't be alarmed. Crank the heat to high and bring to a boil. Once boiling, reduce to medium-high and cook for 10 minutes. If it's popping, cover for a few minutes until it cooks down and stops popping. Stir the beans every minute or so, taking care to scrape the bottom and lift the beans. Meanwhile, slice dark green onion parts

and set aside. After 10 minutes, the beans should have significantly reduced. It may still be a little soupy, but it will thicken as it cools, but if it's really soupy, cook longer. Add hot sauce (or cayenne pepper) to taste if desired. Season with salt and pepper if necessary, stir in leftover green onions, and serve.

PER SERVING

Calories 199, Total Fat 1.9g, Carbohydrates 35.9g, Fiber 9.9g, Sugars 2.6, Protein 10.7g

USA

cajun chickpeas

Straight off of Bourbon Street, these chickpeas are dressed up in Cajun flavoring.

SERVES 2

- 1 14-oz can fire-roasted diced tomatoes
- vegetable broth, as needed
- 1 tbsp tomato paste
- ½ onion, diced
- 1–2 celery stalks, sliced
- 1 green bell pepper, seeded and diced
- 1 tbsp Cajun Seasoning (pg. 230)
- 1 15-oz can chickpeas, drained and rinsed
- hot sauce or cayenne pepper)

Chef's Note Any bell pepper can be used in this recipe, though green is best.

Chef's Note If your Cajun Seasoning is really strong in terms of heat, start at 2 tsp.

Drain tomato juices into a skillet. Add vegetable broth (or water) to the juices so a thin layer of liquid covers the bottom of the skillet. Add diced tomatoes, whisking to combine. Sauté onion, celery, and bell pepper over high heat for 2 minutes, until the bell pepper starts to soften. Add tomato paste and Cajun Seasoning, stirring to combine. Continue to sauté for another 3–4 minutes, until onions are translucent and bell peppers are soft. Turn heat to lowest setting and stir in chickpeas. Cover and let warm for 10–15 minutes, stirring occasionally. (This slow cook helps remove some of the acidic canned tomato flavor. You can add a touch of sugar or other sweetener if it still tastes acidic.) Taste, adding salt and pepper plus hot sauce, such as Tabasco, or cayenne pepper for a spicier dish. Serve over cooked brown rice for a complete meal.

PER SERVING | Calories 273, Total Fat 3.7g, Carbohydrates 46.4g, Fiber 12.3g, Sugars 12.3g, Protein 13.2g

USA

ninny's fruit spring rolls

MAKES 12 ROLLS

- ½ lb tofu, firm
- 1 banana
- ½ apple, sliced
- 12 spring roll wrappers
- 2 large strawberries, chopped
  agave nectar (optional)

DIPPING SAUCE

- 1–2 tbsp peanut butter or vegan chocolate chips
- ¼ c nondairy milk

My sister Courtney (whose nickname is Ninny), brought these rolls over for dessert one day. They were incredible by themselves—but then I got the wild idea to make a peanut butter and chocolate dipping sauce. Heaven!

Press tofu, then cut block into 4 slabs. Cut each slab into 3 pieces, for a total of 12 sticks. Cut banana in half, then slice halves lengthwise. Next, slice each quarter into 3 strips, for a total of 12 banana slices. Slice apple into ⅛ to ¼-inch-wide strips.

Fill a dish or pan with about ¼-inch of water—enough water to cover 1 wrapper. Place 1 spring roll wrapper in cold water for 30–40 seconds (or according to package directions). If the wrapper is not soaked long enough, it is difficult to wrap, and if it is soaked for too long, it can easily tear. Gently take the wrapper out of water dish and let water drain off.

Place wrapper on a flat surface. Place 1 stick of tofu and, 1 slice of banana in the center of the wrapper, and a few slices of strawberry and apple. Drizzle agave on top, if using. Then pick up the bottom of wrapper and fold over the fillings, pick up one side and fold it over, and repeat with the other side. Roll wrapper all the way to the top. Repeat with remaining ingredients.

DIPPING SAUCE

✓ QUICK ✓ GLUTEN-FREE ✓ SOY-FREE ✓ BUDGET ✓ PANTRY

Warm 1–2 tbsp peanut butter in the microwave for a few seconds, then whisk in nondairy milk as necessary to achieve a sauce consistency. Alternatively, melt vegan chocolate chips in the microwave, then whisk in nondairy milk as necessary to achieve a sauce consistency (you may need to reheat).

Chef's Note I place the wrapper on a cutting board with the bottom hanging off of the board. This makes it easier to pick the wrapper up and roll.

PER ROLL
(WITHOUT DIPPING SAUCE)

Calories 120, Total Fat 1.3g, Carbohydrates 22.4g, Fiber 1.2g, Sugars 2.2g, Protein 4.8g

cranberry bread

USA

Cranberry bread is a classic New England treat. I love the tartness of fresh cranberries combined with hints of citrus in this lightly sweet bread. It's perfect for breakfast or served as dessert.

Preheat oven to 350°F. Lightly grease a standard bread pan or line with parchment paper, and set aside. In a large mixing bowl, whisk together flour, baking powder, and baking soda. Add remaining ingredients and stir until just combined. Transfer batter to prepared dish and bake 35–40 minutes.

SERVES 12

- 2 c white whole-wheat flour
- 1 tsp baking powder
- ½ tsp baking soda
- ½ c applesauce
- ¼ c brown or raw sugar
- zest of 1 orange
- 1 tsp vanilla extract
- 1 c nondairy milk
- 1 c sliced cranberries

Chef's Note Slice your cranberries lengthwise.

PER SERVING | Calories 91, Total Fat 0.6g, Carbohydrates 19.5g, Fiber 2.6g, Sugars 5.0g, Protein 2.8g

USA

SERVES 9

pineapple rings

cherries (optional)

brown sugar (optional)

2 c white whole-wheat flour

1 tsp baking powder

½ tsp baking soda

pinch salt (optional)

1 20-oz can crushed pineapple (undrained!)

1 tsp vanilla extract

½ c–1 c raw sugar (see note)

Chef's Note This cake becomes sweeter as it cools.

pineapple upside-down cake

Pineapple upside-down cake is an American classic and one of the few foods I really missed when I switched to a plant-based diet. Now I can have my pineapple cake and eat it too!

Preheat oven to 350°F. Grease a 9-inch cake pan (or use nonstick) and line with pineapple rings, taking care to ensure there is no overlap. Put a cherry in the center of each pineapple ring, if desired. You can also sprinkle the rings with brown sugar if you want your cake to have a glaze-like top. In a medium bowl, whisk together flour, baking powder, baking soda, and a pinch of salt, if desired, until well combined. Then add crushed pineapple with juices, vanilla, and sugar, stirring until just combined. Gently spoon batter into your prepared pan and bake 25–45 minutes, or until a toothpick inserted in the center comes out clean (it usually takes about 35 minutes). Allow to cool, then carefully invert the pan over a plate, and serve.

PER SERVING | Calories 212, Total Fat 0.6g, Carbohydrates 49.7g, Fiber 4.3g, Sugars 28.0g, Protein 4.5g

texas white chili

USA

White chili is traditionally made with white beans and poultry, in comparison to traditional chili that's made with beef in a tomato sauce. I'm using chickpeas instead of poultry in my version, and I added a little Texas-inspired flavor with the salsa verde. For an even hotter version, try adding diced green chilies or jalapeño.

Line a skillet with a thin layer of vegetable broth and sauté onions and garlic over high heat until onions are translucent, about 3 minutes. Add salsa verde and stir to combine. Then add spices and chickpeas, and stir again. Add remaining broth until chili is as juicy as you'd like. Reduce heat to low and continue cooking for a few minutes, until chickpeas are warm. Add salt and white pepper to taste, if desired. Ladle chili into bowls and top with cilantro, green onions, a lime garnish, and a dollop of yogurt if you want to mellow out the heat. You can also break corn chips into the chili for a fuller meal.

SERVES 2

- 1 c vegetable broth
- ⅓ onion, diced
- 3 garlic cloves, minced
- ¾ c salsa verde
- ¼ tsp chili powder
- ½ tsp ground cumin
- ½ tsp coriander
- ½ tsp dried oregano
- 1 15-oz can chickpeas, drained and rinsed

OPTIONAL GARNISHES
**green onions, sliced
cilantro, chopped
lime, thinly sliced
plain vegan yogurt
broken corn chips**

Chef's Note Salsa verde is made of tomatillos, onions, cilantro, and lime. You can find it in the ethnic section of most supermarkets.

PER SERVING | Calories 253, Total Fat 4.6g, Carbohydrates 38g, Fiber 9.8g, Sugar 4.3g, Protein 14.7g

decadent brownies

PRONUNCIATION TIP
Kladdkaka (see Chef's Note) sounds like "kloud-ko-kah."

I love these brownies piping hot out of the oven. They're a richer and more decadent version of my Black Bean Brownies from *The Happy Herbivore Cookbook*.

Preheat oven to 350°F and grease a 9-inch square pan or line with parchment paper and set aside. In a large mixing bowl, whisk Oat Flour, cocoa, baking powder, brown sugar, coffee, and salt, if desired, until well combined, and set aside. Heat chocolate chips in microwave for 20–40 seconds, just until they are soft, not totally melted. Combine chocolate with applesauce, beans, blueberries, and vanilla in a food processor or blender and puree until smooth. Add wet mixture to flour mixture and stir to combine. It will look too dry at first—it's not; keep stroking until you have a thick and shiny batter. If it looks dry (dusted with flour), add a splash of nondairy milk, but you should not need it; keep stroking. Pour batter into prepared pan and bake for 20 minutes.

SERVES 9

- 1 c Oat Flour (pg. 234)
- ¼ c unsweetened cocoa
- ½ tsp baking powder
- 1 c light brown sugar
- 1 packet instant coffee (optional)
- ⅓ c vegan chocolate chips
- ½ c unsweetened applesauce
- ⅓ c canned black beans (drained and rinsed)
- ½ c blueberries (if frozen, thawed)
- 1½ tsp vanilla extract

Chef's Note Although brownies are very American, they are similar to a gooey Swedish cake called *Kladdkaka*, which is also known as chocolate mud cake.

PER SERVING
(WITHOUT COFFEE)

Calories 174, Total Fat 3g, Carbohydrates 35.4g, Fiber 3.5g, Sugars 21.5g, Protein 3.7g

Barcelona is extraordinarily beautiful with the architecture you expect of Spain, but I fell in love with the energy of the city. There is just something about Barcelona that makes every cell in your body pulse and remind you that you are alive. In this moment. Living.

appendix

glossary of ingredients

AGAVE NECTAR

Pronounced ah-GAH-vay, agave nectar is a natural, unrefined sweetener with a consistency similar to honey. It comes from the agave plant, which also is used to make tequila. It can replace honey, sugar, and maple syrup in recipes and works especially well as a sweetener in drinks.

APPLE CIDER VINEGAR

This very acidic and strong-smelling vinegar is made from apples or cider. It is often combined with nondairy milk to sour it into vegan buttermilk. It's also used for flavor and served instead of ketchup with sweet potato fries. Apple cider vinegar can be found in most grocery stores, but you can substitute lemon juice if necessary.

BROTHS

Use any light-colored vegetable broth from bouillon or homemade (pg. 238). When possible, buy no-salt-added or low-sodium options.

BROWN RICE

Bran and germ—key nutrients in rice—have been removed to make white rice white, but brown rice is what white rice once was. To save time, stock up on precooked brown rice that reheats in about a minute.

CHICKPEA FLOUR

Also called garbanzo bean flour and besan, chickpea flour is a light yellow flour made from chickpeas. It's gluten free and provides an egglike taste in cooking.

CHINESE 5-SPICE

Chinese 5-spice is a blend of spices, most commonly cinnamon, star anise, anise seed, ginger, and cloves. It can be found in Asian markets and the Asian section of most grocery stores.

COCOA

Most unsweetened cocoa powders are accidentally vegan. Hershey's and Ghirardelli are good brands to try.

COLLARD GREENS

These leafy greens are an excellent source of fiber and vitamin C. Find them at health food stores and most well-stocked supermarkets. When preparing the greens, be sure to remove the ribs by running a sharp knife along each side.

CONFECTIONERS' SUGAR

Powdered sugar.

COOKING SPRAY

An aerosol designated as a high-heat cooking spray or an oil spray can filled with high-heat cooking oil.

GRANULATED ONION AND GARLIC POWDERS

Look for onion and garlic powders that are granulated, resembling the consistency of fine salt, and not powders that are similar to flour or confectioners' sugar (the latter are sometimes called California-style spices).

INDIAN SPICES

Indian spices such as turmeric, coriander, garam masala, cumin, curry powder, and fennel seeds can be found in most health food stores but are very inexpensive at Indian stores and online.

ITALIAN SEASONING

Italian seasoning is a blend of basil, rosemary, thyme, sage, marjoram, and oregano. In a pinch, Poultry Seasoning Mix (p. 232) can be substituted.

KALE

This leafy green is an excellent source of antioxidants, beta carotene, vitamins K and C, and calcium. Kale can be found at health food stores and most well-stocked supermarkets. I prefer the dark, deep green Lacinato kale commonly labeled dinosaur kale. When preparing kale, be sure to remove the ribs by running a sharp knife along each side.

KELP

A deepwater sea vegetable that's high in iodine but low in sodium (salt), kelp also gives food a fishy taste and is the key to making vegan versions of fish foods. Kelp usually comes in the form of flakes or granules in a small shaker container. You can find it in the Asian section of health food stores or online.

LIQUID SMOKE

Found in most supermarkets, liquid smoke is smoke condensation captured in water. It looks like low-sodium soy sauce but smells like barbecue.

MISO

Found in the refrigerated food section of health food stores and Asian supermarkets, miso is usually made from soybeans, although it can also be made from rice, barley, wheat, or chickpeas.

MORI-NU TOFU

This shelf-stable tofu can be found in the Asian section of most grocery stores, but it is sometimes also kept with produce. Buy Mori-Nu Lite if possible.

NONDAIRY MILK

Soy milk, rice milk, hemp milk, oat milk, and almond milk are just some of the many kinds of nondairy milk on the market. West-Soy makes a fat-free soy milk, but many other brands make light nondairy milks that have a marginal amount of fat. These milks can be used interchangeably in recipes, so feel free to use any type of milk you enjoy or have on hand.

NUTRITIONAL YEAST

Nutritional yeast is a deactivated yeast, meaning it doesn't make breads rise the way active yeast does. Nutritional yeast is a complete protein, low in fat and sodium, and fortified with vitamin B12. It also gives food a cheesy flavor. Nutritional yeast can be found at health food stores and vitamin retailers like GNC and the Vitamin Shoppe. I highly recommend Red Star brand, which can be found in some stores and bought in bulk online.

POULTRY SEASONING

Poultry seasoning is a blend of basil, rosemary, thyme, sage, marjoram, and oregano, but other herbs can be included from time to time. Avoid buying powdered poultry spice or chicken spice rubs, which can be salty. Look for a granulated poultry spice or make your own blend using the recipe on pg. 232.

POWDERED SUGAR

Also called confectioners' sugar, powdered sugar is very fine and powder-like. You can make your own by combining 1 cup of raw sugar with 2 tablespoons of cornstarch in your food processor and letting the motor run until a fine powder is formed.

PUMPKIN PIE SPICE

This blend of cinnamon, ginger, cloves, and nutmeg gives pumpkin pie and other pumpkin foods that distinct flavor we know and love.

PURE MAPLE SYRUP

Pure maple syrup is a delicious natural, unrefined sweetener. Imitation maple syrups and pancake syrups cannot be substituted without sacrificing taste and quality. Agave nectar can be substituted for pure maple syrup, but the taste will be different.

PURE PUMPKIN

Pure pumpkin is different from pumpkin pie mix (don't use that). You want canned pure pumpkin or the insides of an actual pumpkin. In a pinch, you can substitute canned sweet potato or potato squash.

QUINOA

Although technically a pseudo-cereal, quinoa is commonly treated as a grain. It has a nutty flavor and is full of calcium, iron, and magnesium. Quinoa is also a complete protein and cooks quickly, making it a perfect substitute for rice, oatmeal, and other grains when your time is limited. Most U.S. brands of quinoa have been prerinsed, but if your quinoa has a chalky coating, rinse it several times before cooking or it will taste very bitter and soapy. Quinoa bought from the bulk bin should always be rinsed before cooking.

RAW SUGAR

Also called turbinado sugar, raw sugar is a natural, unrefined sugar made from cane juice.

SOY YOGURT

Soy yogurt is made from soy instead of dairy. Alternatively, there are also coconut-milk yogurts and rice-milk yogurts. Find them at health food stores.

SPICES (GENERALLY)

If you buy nothing else organic, try to buy organic and premium spices. A crappy spice can ruin an entire meal. Whole Foods Market has a wide variety of organic spices for as little as $1.99 each. If you don't mind buying in bulk, specialty spice shops and online shops offer great deals.

Good brands to try include Rani, Frontier, Swanson, Spice Islands, Spice Hunter, Simply Organic, Penzeys, and Badia.

TAMARI

Interchangeable with low-sodium soy sauce in recipes, tamari is similar to low-sodium soy sauce but thicker and usually gluten-free.

TEMPEH

Essentially, tempeh is fermented soy bean cakes originating from Indonesia. You can find tempeh at health food stores and in well-stocked supermarkets.

TOFU

There are two distinct types of tofu: tofu that is refrigerated and sitting in water, and tofu (such as Mori-Nu) that is packaged in Tetra Paks and is shelf-stable. Tetra Pak–packaged tofu is very soft and delicate. Refrigerated tofu has a much firmer texture, making it a great replacement for meat. There are several kinds of refrigerated tofu: soft or silken, which is delicate; firm; extra-firm; and super-protein, which is

the hardest. The consistency of tofu also changes when it is fried, cooked, baked, or frozen and later thawed.

VEGAN CHOCOLATE CHIPS

Many semisweet chocolate chips are accidentally vegan. Ghirardelli is my favorite brand.

VITAL WHEAT GLUTEN

Gluten is the protein found in wheat. It's what gives bread its shape and pizza dough its elasticity. When steamed, baked, boiled, or otherwise cooked, gluten becomes chewy, with a very meat-like texture, and is referred to as seitan. Gluten also works as a binding agent, helping hold things like mushroom burgers together. You can find vital wheat gluten in the baking section of health food stores or online.

recipe substitutions*

I like to use dried herbs and spices in my recipes because I always have them on hand, they're cheaper, I can save an additional 5 minutes of prep time, and I dirty fewer dishes. I still love fresh ingredients though, especially those I've grown myself, so here is a handy substitution chart if you'd like to use fresh. I can't guarantee the results will be the same, and you may need to do a little tweaking as you go, but in theory these swaps should work fine.

FRESH >> DRIED HERBS

1 tbsp fresh = 1 tsp dried

Note If I use fresh herbs in a recipe, such as with the Quick Pesto (p. 182), dried herbs cannot be substituted.

ONION >> ONION POWDER

1 small onion (⅓ c) = 1 tsp onion powder
1 small onion (⅓ c) = 1 tbsp onion flakes

GARLIC >> GARLIC POWDER

1 clove = ½ tsp minced garlic
1 clove = ¼ tsp garlic powder (granulated)
1 clove = ⅛ tsp garlic powder (flour consistency)

LEMON >> LEMON JUICE

1 lemon = 2–3 tbsp lemon juice
1 lemon wedge = ¼–1 tsp lemon juice

Note Fresh lemon juice is much more potent than store-bought juices. Use fresh whenever possible, adding lemon or lime juice from a bottle to taste.

*INFORMATION COURTESY OF THE COOK'S THESAURUS, WWW.FOODSUBS.COM

DRIED BEANS >> CANNED BEANS

1¼–1¾ c cooked beans = 15 oz canned beans

SUGAR REPLACEMENT

You can safely reduce sugar by ¼ in any recipe, or use these other sweeteners instead of sugar:

REPLACEMENT FOR 1 CUP OF SUGAR	ADDITIONAL CHANGES
¾ c barley malt syrup	Reduce liquid by ¼
⅔ c date sugar	(no reduction)
1 c fruit syrup	Reduce liquid by ¼
1 c pure maple syrup	Reduce liquid by 3 tbsp, add ¼ tsp baking soda
1 c Sucanat	(no reduction)
1 tsp powdered stevia	(no reduction)

TIP Take care with substitutions and adaptations. When making a change, ask yourself, "What does the original ingredient do? Does my substitute have the same texture, taste, consistency, color and feel as the original?" Sometimes changing one thing changes everything.

Madrid, Spain (2011)

kitchen prep lingo

I remember my early days in the kitchen. They were filled with questions like "How small is a small onion?" or "What is the difference between mince and chop?" To help cut back on your Google searches, I've created this cheat sheet of terms you'll run across in this cookbook.

ALMOST COMBINED/JUST COMBINED
Do not completely combine ingredients. With batter, some flour should still be visible for it to be almost combined. To be just combined, stir it just a little bit more— ingredients should be mixed together and are incorporated, but barely. Use as few strokes as possible. (Compare with *Blend.*)

BEANS
Use canned beans, drained and rinsed, unless the recipe specifically calls for dried beans.

BLEND
Stir to incorporate all ingredients until they are well combined and the mix is homogenous.

CHOP
Cut ingredient into bite-size pieces; uniform cuts are not necessary, and size is relatively unimportant (it's more of a personal preference).

COOKED
A vegetable prepared by steaming, baking, or boiling until fork-tender (seeded and/or skinned prior to cooking if necessary).

CREAM
Beat the ingredients with an electric mixer until they are well combined and have a creamy consistency. This also can be done by hand with a spatula.

CRUMBLE
Break the ingredient apart into smaller pieces. With tofu, break the tofu apart until it resembles ricotta or feta cheese.

FOLD
Gently stir a single ingredient into a mixture, such as muffin batter, with a spatula or large spoon until just combined.

LINE (WITH WATER OR BROTH)

Add a thin layer of liquid that just barely covers the bottom of the pot or skillet. Start with $1/4$ cup.

MINCE

Chop ingredients into very small pieces, $1/8$ inch or smaller.

ONION

Small onions are the size of a lemon, medium onions are roughly the size of an orange, and large onions are the size of a grapefruit.

SALT AND PEPPER TO TASTE

$1/2$ teaspoon of salt and $1/4$ teaspoon of pepper is usually a good starting point for recipes that serve at least two. Reduce salt if you're using ingredients with sodium, such as canned goods or low-sodium soy sauce. Double as necessary to achieve your preferred taste.

STIR

Use a circular motion, clockwise or counterclockwise, to move or incorporate ingredients.

metric conversions

ABBREVIATION KEY

tsp = teaspoon
tbsp = tablespoon
dsp = dessert spoon

U.S. STANDARD	U.K.
¼ tsp	¼ tsp (scant)
½ tsp	½ tsp (scant)
¾ tsp	½ tsp (rounded)
1 tsp	¾ tsp (slightly rounded)
1 tbsp	2½ tsp
¼ cup	¼ cup minus 1 dsp
⅓ cup	¼ cup plus 1 tsp
½ cup	⅓ cup plus 2 dsp
⅔ cup	½ cup plus 1 tbsp
¾ cup	½ cup plus 2 tbsp
1 cup	¾ cup plus 2 dsp

index

O

Oat Flour   234
Oats
    in Lentil Loaf   257
    in Müesli   134
    in No-Meat "Meatballs"   181
Olives
    in Insalata Fantasia   111
    in Mediterranean Chard   67
    in Nona's Chickpeas   51
    in Pesto-Stuffed Mushrooms   99
Olive Tapenade   206
    in Spaghetti alla Puttanesca   173
Onions
    in African Delight   106
    in African Jollof   129
    in Aloo Gobi   109
    in Aloo Matar   102
    in Bavarian Onion Soup   33
    in Bolognese Sauce   168
    in Cajun Chickpeas   274
    in Cajun Stuffed Mushrooms   258
    in Carolina Casserole   265
    in Cassoulet   18
    in "Cheater" African Green
       Beans   231
    in "Cheater" Romesco Sauce   170
    in Chickpea Cacciatore   45
    in Cuban Black Bean Soup   17
    in Drunken Beans   49
    in Edamame   81
    in German Lentil Soup   14
    in German Potato Salad   63
    in Lentil Loaf   257
    in Mama D's Spanakorizo   120
    in Masoor Dal   46
    in Moroccan Vegetables   105
    in Mushroom Broth   235
    in No-Meat "Meatballs"   181
    in Quick Chili Mole   27
    in Saag   62
    in Skillet Green Bean Casserole   270
    in Stuffed Poblanos   96
    in Swedish Split Pea Soup   24
    in Texas White Chili   281
    in Vegetable Broth   238
    in Vegetable Enchiladas   103
    in Vegetable Korma   100
Onion Soup, Bavarian   33
Orange
    in Morir Soñando   219
    in Sangria   217
    in Winter Confetti Salad   267
Orange juice, in Morir Soñando   219
Orange soda, in Tinto de Verano   215
Orange Teriyaki Rice   130

P

Pad Thai
    "Cheater"   178
    Lower-Calorie   179
    Vegetable   179
Paella   127
Parsnip
    in Vegetable Broth   238
    in Winter Confetti Salad   267
Pasta
    "Cheater" Pad Thai   178
    Gin's Gnocchi   174
    Lasagna   177
    Lower-Calorie Pad Thai   179
    Pasta e Fagioli   176
    Spaghetti alla Puttanesca   173
    Thai Noodle Soup   29
    Vegetable Pad Thai   179
Pasta e Fagioli   176
Patatas Bravas   68
Peanut butter
    in "Cheater" African Green
       Beans   231
    in "Cheater" Tofu Satay   196
    in Dipping Sauce   277
Peas
    in Aloo Matar   102
    in Vegetable Korma   100
Peppered Mushroom Gravy   262
Pesto
    Chermoula (Moroccan Pesto)   197
    Quick   182
Pesto-Stuffed Mushrooms   99
Pilaf, Roasted Tomato   124
Pineapple

acknowledgments

I feel thankful every day for the support of my fans (called Herbies). I would not have the opportunity to write cookbooks if it was not for them. Herbies, everything I do, I do for you.

I would also like to acknowledge the team behind this book: **Amy Sly**, thank you for giving me such a beautiful book; **Nichelle Nicholes**, thank you for editing and proofing my manuscript—goodness knows you had your hands full; and **Leigh Camp**, thank you for managing the entire project. I would also like to thank my sister, **Courtney Hardy**, who was by my side through the entire book, doing everything and anything I asked. I absolutely could not have finished this book without you.

A special thank you to my husband, **Scott Nixon**, who pushes me through to the very end and never lets me quit. *Happy Herbivore Abroad* would not exist without your unwavering support and determination. Additionally, thank you to the many Herbies who checked my pronunciations and translations.

Lastly, my wonderful group of testers who took on the collective nickname of **Tofu Rangers**—there is no way I could have written this book without your feedback and support!

Erin Almond

Jared Bigman

Courtney Blair

Sheree Britt

Lisa Canada and Family

Leslie Conn

Jessica "Tofessica" Creech

Candy Guerra

Jennifer Kent

Amanda Martin

Kim Michael

Ashley and Michael Nebel

Nichelle Nicholes

Elena Paulsen

Gayle Pollick

Elisabeth Redman

Tara-Lynn Reidy

Kaitlyn B Scalisi

Gin Stafford

Laura Jill "LJ" Steinig

Dana Strickland

Diane Wilson Thomas

Brenna & Delaney Treanor (with parents)

Roxanne Veinotte

Lisa Yost

Andrea Dermos

about the author

Lindsay S. Nixon is a rising star in the culinary world, praised for her ability to use everyday ingredients to create healthy, low-fat recipes that taste just as delicious as they are nutritious. Nixon's recipes have been featured in the *New York Times*, *Vegetarian Times*, *Women's Health* magazine, and on The Huffington Post as well as countless vegan/vegetarian blogs. Nixon's work has been praised and endorsed by notable leaders in the plant-based movement such as Dr. T. Colin Campbell, Dr. Caldwell Esselstyn, Dr. Neal Barnard, and Dr. John Mc-Dougall. You can learn more about Nixon and sample some of her recipes at HappyHerbivore.com.

ready to travel?

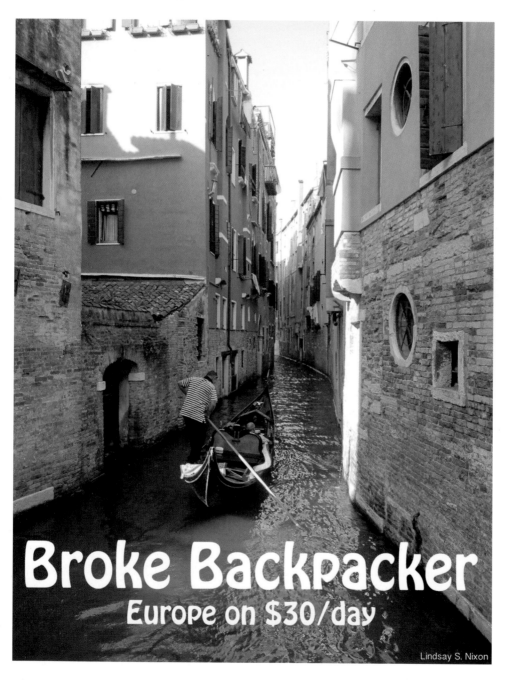

Broke Backpacker
Europe on $30/day

Lindsay S. Nixon

For more information visit brokebackpackerbook.com.